IPSE DIXIT

WILLIAM L. DWYER

Foreword by Meade Emory / Introduction by Stimson Bullitt

THE UNIVERSITY OF WASHINGTON SCHOOL OF LAW

IPSE DIXIT

How the World Looks to a Federal Judge

UNIVERSITY OF WASHINGTON PRESS *SEATTLE & LONDON*

© 2007 by the University of Washington Press

Printed in the United States of America

Design by Audrey Seretha Meyer

12 11 10 09 08 07   5 4 3 2 1

University of Washington Press

P.O. Box 50096, Seattle, WA 98145

www.washington.edu/uwpress

Library of Congress Cataloging-in-Publication Data

Dwyer, William L.

    Ipse dixit : how the world looks to a federal judge / William L.
Dwyer ; foreword by Meade Emory ; introduction by Stimson
Bullitt.

      p. cm.

Includes bibliographical references and index.

ISBN-13: 978-0-295-98704-0 (hardback : alk. paper)

ISBN-10: 0-295-98704-9 (hardback : alk. paper)

1. Judges—United States.   2. Lawyers—United States.

3. Practice of law—United States. I. Title.

KF8775.D89   2007

347.73'14—dc22   2007002326

The paper used in this publication is acid-free and 90 percent recycled
from at least 50 percent post-consumer waste. It meets the minimum
requirements of American National Standard for Information Sciences—
Permanence of Paper for Printed Library Materials, ANSI Z39.48–1984.

To my grandchildren

Maxwell, Henry, Sam, Nicholas, and Ella

Contents

Foreword

MEADE EMORY

S EVERAL TIMES IN MY LEGAL CAREER MY PATH HAS intersected with William Dwyer's. I was asked in 1986 to testify before the Senate Judiciary Committee in support of his nomination as a U.S. District Court judge for the Western District of Washington. Because I have greatly admired Bill Dwyer throughout my professional life, I enthusiastically seized the opportunity to do so. When University of Washington Law School Dean Roland Hjorth decided to create a faculty chair bearing Dwyer's name, the School's Graduate Program in Taxation, of which I was then director, contributed substantially to the chair's endowment fund. The William L. Dwyer Chair in Law was dedicated in 2001, and the first and current occupant is my colleague Stewart Jay. Following Judge Dwyer's death in 2002, it was learned that he had decided not to archive his papers but to let his judicial decisions and opinions speak for themselves. Thus, when it became known that he had left a varied and wide-ranging collection of speeches given during his distinguished career, I was enormously pleased to help facilitate publication of this important legacy of Bill Dwyer.

Anyone who has followed Bill Dwyer's career, both before and after he went on the bench, knows that somehow he was at the center of this region's most difficult legal issues. When he was in private practice, his noteworthy cases included a libel suit on behalf of John Goldmark, an Okanogan County legislator and rancher, against detractors who had accused Goldmark of Communist sympathies; representation of King County in a dispute with the builder who defaulted on the contract to build the Kingdome in Seattle; pro bono representation of newspaper employees contesting the proposed joint-operating agreement between the Seattle Times and the Seattle Post-Intelligencer; and a suit against the American League that resulted in Dwyer becoming known as the lawyer who brought baseball back to Seattle. The scope and significance of these matters can be attributed to his courage and to the fact that his excellent reputation at the bar brought clients with the most challenging issues to his doorstep.

Since cases are assigned to sitting federal judges on a random basis, the fact that Judge Dwyer's docket drew an inordinate number of the Northwest's truly weighty issues cannot be explained. However, how he dealt with the legal complexity and potentially groundbreaking nature of these cases is permanently writ large on the jurisprudential history of our region. Among the most significant issues that found their way to his court were the spotted owl cases, brought by the Seattle Audubon Society, in which Dwyer ordered the Forest Service to adopt a plan substantially reducing logging in owl habitat areas. The decision in these cases posited our society's fundamental struggle between its ecological conscience and its need to get goods and services from the land. Other issues included a decision declaring Washington State's term-limit law for elected officials unconstitutional because it restricted voters' freedom of choice; a ruling that

Metro (King County's transportation and public utility authority) as then structured was unconstitutional; and, after lengthy hearing, his order—compliance with which he closely monitored—requiring state officials to provide adequate mental-health care for civilly committed sex offenders.

An essential reason why Dean Hjorth was eager to create the Dwyer Chair in Law, and why I and others in the Law School were so pleased to honor Judge Dwyer's memory through the publication of these memorable speeches, was Dwyer's love of the legal profession. His profound interest in and respect for legal education went so far as to prompt him to design and teach a course on the history and philosophy of litigation at the Law School, a rare task for any busy practitioner to consider, let alone bring off with stunning success. This devotion clearly manifested itself in Judge Dwyer's remarks at the dedication of the Chair being named for him, at which time he spoke of the legal profession's "camaraderie, its challenges, its opportunities for adventure, and its ever renewed invitation to give the best that is in us." While Judge Dwyer recalled the utility of the Socratic method in learning "how to think like a lawyer," he correctly noted that the legal education formula at the time he went to law school was "weak on the big picture," whereas today's "course catalog reads like a fascinating itinerary through the wide world of the law." Dwyer noted that in his days at the UW Law School, the student body and faculty were "composed almost entirely of white males," and he heralded the winds of change that brought about real diversity, noting that in the early twenty-first century, for example, "half the students are women and about a fourth are minorities."

Observing that up to three-fourths of the "legal needs of poor Americans go unmet" and that the legal profession's members need "to give generously of their time and talent" to remedy the situation, Dwyer noted that "most of us are too busy," adding, pivotally, "or think we are." His shrewd knowledge of the profession was evident in his statement that as "lawyers and judges we habitually concentrate on the work at hand—the trial in progress, the document to be drafted, the negotiation to be conducted," rather than seek to comply with the "aspirational statements" of the canon of ethics, which, in his words, urges all members of the bar to donate substantial working time to pro bono services. His knowledge of what goes on in legal education at the University of Washington elicited his comment that its Law School set a "sterling example" when its students a "few years ago . . . voted to impose on themselves a requirement for graduation of at least sixty hours of public service work" and that that program "has been a tremendous success." The strong implication of this is, of course, that if law students can be so motivated, why can't those who are "the stewards and trustees of the legal system," as he put it, do the same?

The speeches collected in this volume are neither dry nor pedantic. Rather, they reveal the breadth and scope of Bill Dwyer's interests and wisdom. No hubris or egotism is displayed in these pages. In this regard much is learned about the kind of man he was from his comment that "once off the bench at the end of the day, it is gratifying to find one's anonymity has survived almost intact." These short but interesting talks also lack histrionics and are marked by the use of the "simple language and infallible logic" that Gordon Culp, Dwyer's longtime law partner, says Dwyer used in daily discourse, both in and out of the courtroom. Judge Robert Lasnik, a colleague on the local federal bench, noted that "there was no hierarchy" for Bill Dwyer, "he was great to everybody." His reputation for fairness, integrity, and intelligence was so broadly recognized that it was perfectly appropriate, in an age rife with lawyer-bashing humor, for Seattle lawyer Egil (Bud) Krogh Jr. to view Bill Dwyer as having "helped redeem our profession" through the respect, bordering on reverence, that he enjoyed.

Friends counted him "as a richly shared experience" (Emmett Watson's words) and felt "rather sorry for people who didn't know him as well as [they] did." His pal Watson also remarked that the "air becomes less troubled when he is around." I expect that the readers of these speeches will have much the same quieting and reassuring reaction.

Bill Dwyer helped the Seattle Public Library reach its conclusion that retaining a certain sex-education book on its noncirculating reserve shelf was not in violation of state or federal law, but his advice in that regard was seized upon by opponents of his confirmation to the bench to portray him as soft on pornography. While this charge was thoroughly and systematically shown to be without any basis, it did have the effect of stretching out the Senate Judiciary Committee's hearing and changing what otherwise would have been an easy confirmation into a bit of an ordeal. With characteristic class and grace, Bill Dwyer said on the final day of his hearing that even "knowing the furor [his work on behalf of the library] has caused," he would take "this assignment again . . . because as soon as you start turning down legal matters out of fear of what they're going to do to your personal career, you might as well hang it up and stop being a practicing lawyer," a statement applauded by Senator Pat Leahy, the Committee's chair, as being in the "finest tradition of the bar."

I hope you feel, as I do, that Bill Dwyer's integrity, wit, and adherence to and respect for the rule of law shine through in this wonderful collection of speeches, a laudable written monument to a man who is greatly missed.

March 2007

Introduction

STIMSON BULLITT

JUDGE WILLIAM DWYER ASSEMBLED SOME OF HIS
speeches for the purpose of publishing them and even wrote a
preface for the planned book in the months before his death in 2002.
The speeches all reflect his belief in the institutions of government
and law and his conclusions drawn from deep thought and experience. The speech-essays included in this book, like the practice of law
itself, also bear on the concerns and collisions that are frequently presented by life and can occasionally bring us into court.

In his address to the Seattle-Nantes Sister City Association, for
example, Dwyer reflected on the contribution to human liberty provided by the French Revolution's Declaration of the Rights of Man.
He examined the development of human rights in light of their dates
of recognition and their protection by governments and courts. He
noted the *Declaration's* asserted right of an individual to own pri-

vate property, a right with a close connection to personal freedom at a time when most private property took the form of farms. He remarked on how international law has been moving beyond issues between nations to include issues within nations and is taking a step toward less tolerance of sovereignty and more willingness to interfere with a nation's denial of freedom to its citizens. The United Nations' Universal Declaration of Human Rights, which presented its principles as a further step toward human liberties, supported this trend.

At a Washington State Library Association conference, Dwyer gave an eloquent tribute to librarians, those who preserve and dispense the language that holds us together and the ideas that link us to our past. In a real sense, the value of libraries and the rights of man reflect the principles upon which Judge Dwyer's life was based.

Dwyer organized his speeches in order of their date of delivery. Rather than end with three memorials to deceased friends, however, he departed from a chronological scheme by closing with two longer speeches that express his belief in and hopes for our legal system, subjects upon which long immersion through reading, thought, and work had made him an expert. Although nonlawyers probably comprised only a small proportion of the audience for these speeches, Dwyer's subject matter and manner of expression do not require legal knowledge to comprehend and appreciate.

In thirty years of trial practice, Bill Dwyer scored many big wins, and winning gave him plenty of pleasure. He loved the law, whether standing before the bench or sitting on it. But his pleasures and interests, if not his ambitions, went beyond scores in court. His family and friends meant much to him. He gave generously of himself to them and took pride in them. In this, he contrasted with Epaminondas, the great Greek general who, as he lay dying, childless, boasted that he had victories for daughters. Bill Dwyer's personality enabled him to shift effortlessly between sparkling levity among companions and sober dignity while on the bench.

His interests beyond the law extended in several directions. He taught a course on the history and philosophy of litigation; he took a year off to live in Spain; and he and his wife traveled the world and were active at home in Seattle's arts community. He played the judge in the play *Inherit the Wind*, which dramatized the Scopes trial. He composed—wholly in palindromes—the libretto for a romantic opera, with characters including La Paloma Amola Pal and her dog Fifi. He and Emmett Watson owned an oyster bar in the Pike Place Market. Watson once wrote of him, "Giving Bill Dwyer the shallow label of 'liberal' is to say of a melody that it amounts to a symphony. There are many bars of music that make the man. . . . And always, of course, there is the pleasure of his company. The air becomes less troubled when he is around. Good things happen when he is near."

Dwyer's friends came from all walks and levels of life. In his law practice, he had many facets. Some people nicknamed him Destructo for the way he took apart hostile witnesses with his soft-spoken and polite questioning. As both an advocate and a judge, he used persistent diplomatic skills to bring to pass the settlement of heated and expensive disputes.

William Dwyer was born on March 26, 1929. His mother was a secretary and his father, a truck driver; when he was five, his parents divorced and William went to live with his mother. It has been said that he played during his school years, but perhaps it would be more accurate to say he was unfocused. He worked at outside jobs while going through law school and still made the staff of the University of Washington *Law Review*—only the most brilliant of playboys can do that. Both ambitious and successful in his rise as a lawyer, he nevertheless "didn't win 'em all." Not until his second try was he elected president of his city-county bar association.

Despite his successes, he was modest, as is illustrated in this collection of speeches and in his two previously published books. None is self-promoting. In his book *The Goldmark Case*, the tale of a political trial in Okanogan County, Dwyer made his client, John Goldmark, the central character, although the facts would have supported titling the book "One of My Most Magnificent Triumphs." A Seattle lawyer who acknowledges that he wouldn't presume to share anything of Bill Dwyer's save a chronically bad lower back commented, "I'm neither proud nor ashamed of most of the advice I've offered others over the years, because so little of it was followed. But I'm proud to have advised John Goldmark to retain young Bill Dwyer, only ten years after his admission to the bar."

In the Hands of the People, published just before Dwyer's death at age seventy-two, examines the jury system in comparison to bench trials and other systems. The author's knowledge, experience, judgment, and clarity educate the reader and do so without illustrating his points with displays of his past victories or prowess. Some of Dwyer's friends have wondered if his string of victories might have whispered in his ear: "My cases were just causes. Juries held for my clients. Ergo, the jury system is the best engine for justice." If this syllogism had been expressly posed to him, the judge would have recognized it as false and rejected it with a smile and a quip.

His transparent integrity was illustrated repeatedly in his testimony before the Senate Judiciary Committee when it considered his nomination for the U.S. District Court bench. His confirmation proceedings were contested over a period of a year and a half. Widespread expressions of admiration and approval were somewhat offset by hostile assertions that he was not qualified and would be a disgrace as a judge.

A carefully reasoned opinion explaining one of Bill Dwyer's decisions was described by a timber industry lobbyist as "14 pages of diatribal discourse." And a representative for contract loggers complained that the judge got to "play the role of God in the Pacific Northwest." Some ardent members of the movement to protect children from molestation contended that he was "soft on child pornography" (and a flaming civil libertarian, to boot). This epithet stemmed from his role in advising his client, the Seattle Public Library Board, on the legality of keeping a sex-education manual titled *Show Me!* on the library's shelves. When board members asked him if the library would be committing a crime to keep the book in its collection, he advised them that it would not. This advice caught the eye and the fancy of Senator Strom Thurmond, who combined a dislike for pornography with a dislike for the kind of public figure exemplified by Bill Dwyer.

A second hot button for his opponents was Dwyer's apparent criticism in *The Goldmark Case* of right-wing supporters of Goldmark's calumniators. Dwyer testified about what he had written:

> Senator [Thurmond], . . . I just describe what happened. And it is a fact, which we would be remiss if we didn't face, that there have been periods in our history when anti-Communism has become inflamed, over-aggressive, and unrealistic in its descriptions of what is going on in the country and the world.
>
> To some extent, we went through such a period in the early 1960s, especially while John Kennedy was president. The reason I mentioned any of that in this book is that it is a prelude, it sets the stage for the libel of John Goldmark and the trial that followed.

Strom Thurmond tried to pry out of Dwyer some acknowledgment of falsehood about, or disloyalty to, Ronald Reagan, the man who had nominated him for U.S. District Court. When Thurmond persisted with the question, Did you support him for president? after colloquy, Dwyer testified, "I supported Mr. Mondale in the 1984 election, and in 1980 I supported President Carter."

Illustrating his humor and his nerve, when he met Supreme Court

Justice Sandra Day O'Connor at a reception during a break in the vetting process, he asked her about the truth of a story he had heard: Justice O'Connor and her two most elderly colleagues had shared a meal in the Court dining room. She had ordered a main course, when the waiter asked, "And what about the vegetables?" She allegedly replied, "The vegetables will have to order for themselves." To Bill's question, O'Connor just smiled.

His humor could just as often be directed at himself. He won a complex construction contract case, the trial of which took five months. When he spoke to an audience of law students about that trial, he used it as an occasion to advise them that lawyers should be brief: The judge in the case had been in the audience at another event where Dwyer was the speaker and had told him, "You know, as soon as I heard your voice tonight, I started to fall asleep."

Although he was always aggressive as an advocate for those he represented and was filled with energy for the institutions he cherished, Bill Dwyer did little to promote himself. He often attributed his successes to luck and gifts of good fortune, as he did on the occasion of being presented with an endowed chair in his name at the University of Washington School of Law.

His capacity to enjoy his pursuit of intellectual, social, and cultural interests while at the same time achieving great career success inspired awe and envy in those of us who wished we could do the same. He and his wife, Vasiliki, took long trips abroad and spent time in their vacation home on the coast of Mexico. I'll admit that most of my own good times with Bill Dwyer took place indoors, but in the mountains we enjoyed some memorable pleasures, too. Even though he was a better tennis player than mountaineer, Bill was an enthusiast for the Cascades. On a hike to Chimney Rock with Bill and Charles Goldmark, our three families intertwined, "the sun shone bright, and the birds made music all the day." Years later, after Chuck Goldmark's death, Chuck's nephew, Jesse, and Bill Dwyer circumnavigated Eight-Mile Lake above Icicle Creek.

One particularly memorable day, Shelby Scates, Joan Hansen, Bill, and I set forth into the North Cascades, when suddenly the weather turned to dense, damp fog. We went up to Cascade Pass, then south a bit where we camped beside an obscure little pond dignified on the map as Cool Ade Lake. Shelby and Joan had brought a tent. Bill and I had not. Rain fell hard all night. By chance, my resting place resembled an upside-down butter dish; Bill's was more like the butter dish itself. After his site had filled with water and he had floated for a while, desperation drove him to the door of the small tent, which he entered as if he were a big, wet dog. The next morning, peering through the mist, we hiked out dispiritedly. On our last mountain excursion together before lung cancer took its toll on Bill, we roamed from Rainy Pass to Heather Pass, Black Peak, and Maple Pass.

Only those deficient in observation or human sympathy contend that life itself is simple. But some remarkable people can express, in terms that are simple and clear, the complexity that bears on all our lives. Judge Dwyer's writings are like that, beautiful and clear. He never wrote to display his learning; he wrote because "the work all of us do in the law is at the surfline of a deep sea of history that must be explored if we are to understand the tides and the breakers and the weather on shore." And his self-deprecating humor—graceful and elegant and generous with compliments—contributes to our high opinion of the man and to the pleasure in reading his thoughts.

William Dwyer inspired both admiration and devotion. A week before he died, I wrote to Bill:

A few more thoughts . . . about you. You have a fine mind and other gifts and merits, but your most notable feature is your character. Over my life, longer than yours, I've never met a finer man. Mentioned because it comes to mind rather than because of its importance, an appealing aspect of your values is that, unlike some others who can do so, you don't confine your guest list to the brilliant and the eminent. Your nobility of spirit has elevated my life.

The public addresses published here reflect a life well lived. They provide instruction and understanding, stating and explaining as they do their author's values as well as his opinions and keen insights. The reader will take pleasure from the good writings of William Dwyer.

March 2007

IPSE DIXIT

Preface

THIS BOOK IS A SAMPLING OF SPEECHES I HAVE given during my years as a federal judge. I have put it together—"written it" would not be right, since the speeches had already been reduced to writing—for two categories of readers. The first group is those who might be curious about what I, and others of a similar cast of mind, have thought about, worried over, and laughed at near the turn of the twenty-first century. The second group is my grandchildren and others of their vintage, who are too young to understand but with whom I feel an irresistible desire to communicate. For them, the time to read these pages might be ten or fifteen years from now.

I have kept the sampling brief—it includes just a little more than a dozen speeches, some of them very short—and have omitted subjects that are dealt with in my earlier books, *The Goldmark Case* and *In the Hands of the People.*

As the reader will see, the speeches reflect faith in the intelligence and honor of ordinary men and women, confidence in the central values of the Anglo-American legal system, and optimism over our collective ability—if we use our heads—to survive and to let the rest of life survive with us. These beliefs, of course, cannot be proved true in the way that a scientific proposition can be proved. I can only say that they stem from long experience, that I profoundly believe them to be right, and that holding them is a lot more enjoyable than giving way to pessimism. Beyond that, it is simply a case of *ipse dixit*—"It's true because I say it's true."

W. L. D.
December 2001

Remarks at the Federal Bar Association

BANQUET HONORING JUDGE GEORGE H. BOLDT

July 26, 1978

IT IS AN HONOR TO SPEAK HERE TONIGHT, EVEN AS a substitute. Bill Helsell's first official act as the new president of the Seattle-King County Bar Association was to get on a ship and sail away to Australia.[1] He will be gone for six weeks. This marks a new pace in conducting the affairs of our Association, which we all look forward to following in the coming year.

It is fitting that we pause now to reflect on how Judge Boldt arrived at this remarkable point in his career,[2] and why all of us have come to honor him tonight. The story of his life is worth considering—because it tells a good deal about our country, as well as about our honored guest.

Not many people know that George Boldt came from an immigrant background. His father immigrated to the United States from Sweden. His mother was the daughter of immigrant parents from Denmark. Their son came from the kind of background that, so often in our country, has produced great results. Judge Boldt has said that his most precious possession is his father's certificate of naturalization as an American citizen. That was issued in 1896.

George Boldt was born in 1903. He grew up in Montana and has never completely lost the traces of that Montana origin, as shown in some of the more vivid parts of his speech. His mother died when he was only thirteen. He progressed through school under difficult conditions, went to the University of Montana, and earned his law degree there in 1926.

Judge Boldt entered private practice at Helena, Montana, in 1926—27. He practiced law in Seattle from 1927 to 1945. He is still a member of the Seattle-King County Bar Association. From 1945 to 1953, he practiced in Tacoma. Many of us still remember the name of his firm: Metzger, Blair, Gardner & Boldt.[3]

Boldt earned a reputation as one of the best trial lawyers in the State of Washington—known for his integrity, native ability, and plain hard work. He handled some famous cases. One of them involved the collapse of the original Tacoma Narrows Bridge, for which he served as Special Assistant Attorney General and achieved an outstanding result for his client, the state of Washington.

In the period from 1942 to 1945, Boldt interrupted his legal career to serve in the Armed Forces of the United States. He served with the OSS in Burma, achieved the rank of lieutenant colonel, and was decorated with the distinguished-unit citation of three battle stars.

In 1953, he was appointed a U.S. District court judge by President Dwight Eisenhower. George Boldt has now served in that capacity, with distinction, for twenty-five years.

While handling a heavy caseload in Tacoma, Judge Boldt has assisted other federal districts by trying cases all over the United States. I will mention just a few of the many important cases over which he has presided.

❏ 1956 *United States v. Northern Pacific R.R.* was a landmark antitrust case that is still frequently cited in litigation in that field.[4]

❏ 1958 *United States v. Dave Beck* was a famous case involving alleged federal tax violations.[5]

❏ 1961 *United States v. Mickey Cohen* was a tax fraud trial in the southern district of California that involved a notorious California citizen.[6] (Cohen was even more notorious after the verdict came in.)

❏ 1961–1967 Judge Boldt was one of the principal judges in the electrical equipment antitrust litigation, a nationwide series of consolidated cases involving 1,912 lawsuits and more than 25,000 individual antitrust claims running into the billions of dollars. In all probability, the electrical equipment antitrust cases were the most extensive and complex litigation ever conducted anywhere. And yet all of the claims were finally concluded within six years. To most people that sounds like an almost incredible achievement. To those who know Judge Boldt, well, there was nothing to it!

❏ 1962 In the Southern District of California, Judge Boldt tried *United States v. Carbo*, a case involving extortion in the prize-fight business.[7]

❏ 1970 The "Seattle Seven" case arose from an assault by demonstrators on the federal courthouse in Seattle and terminated in contempt findings at the trial—an unusually difficult and turbulent case.[8]

❏ 1974 *United States v. Washington et al.* involved Indian fishing rights under a series of treaties entered with the tribes decades before.[9] It is often overlooked that this decision was unanimously affirmed by a panel of the U.S. Court of Appeals for the Ninth Circuit. And I for one firmly believe that Judge Boldt's decision will soon be recognized as a landmark in the just and proper resolution of that long-standing problem.

❏ 1970–75 *Labbee v. Wrigley* was a class-action antitrust case brought by farmers, probably the largest of that nature in the United States.[10]

❑ 1974 In Florida, the *Wynn Oil* case was a complicated Sherman Act trial.[11]

❑ Now [1978] The massive sugar industry antitrust litigation is under way in San Francisco.[12]

These cases I have mentioned are only illustrative. Judge Boldt has handled countless cases in every field from bank mergers to narcotics traffic. He has handled them with skill, fairness, a remarkable efficiency, and—perhaps most important—the courage to uphold the law even when it was unpopular to do so.

Somehow he has found time to do a great many other things. He has often served as an appellate court judge on the U.S. Court of Appeals for the Ninth Circuit. In 1971, he received a telephone call and answered "yes" when most other judges would have said "no." The call was from the White House. Judge Boldt at the time was about to enter upon senior status, usually a comfortable position. President Richard Nixon asked that he leave the bench for an unknown period of time to take on a job that everyone knew would be tough, nasty, and full of unforeseen hazards—that of being chairman of the newly formed Pay Board.[13] The federal government had just ordered price and wage freezes for the first time in a number of years. The job was obviously difficult and unpredictable. That is why Judge Boldt took it. And he not only took it, he achieved in a period of sixteen months' service in Washington an outstanding success in this new and challenging field.

The Judge has also represented the United States at the United Nations Congress on the prevention of crime, held in Geneva, Switzerland. He has served as editor and coauthor of the *Manual for Complex Litigation*, a work that has become a kind of bible for lawyers and judges handling complex cases all over the country. He is a member of the Board of Trustees of the University of Montana and is chairman of the Board of Visitors of the University of Puget Sound Law School.[14] He has served on numerous committees of the federal bar, the American Bar Association, the American Law Institute, and other organizations.

It is no exaggeration to say that Judge Boldt has worked as hard and achieved as much as any district court judge—not just in the United States but in the history of the United States. And he has done all this while keeping the friendship of the lawyers and of many other citizens here in western Washington.

Thinking about Judge Boldt's anniversary tonight, I was reminded of something that Chief Justice Charles Evans Hughes of the United States Supreme Court said back in 1936: "The highest reward that can come to a lawyer is the esteem of his professional brethren. That esteem ... proceeds from an impartial judgment. ... It cannot be purchased. It cannot be artificially created. It cannot be gained by artifice or contrivance to attract public attention. It is not measured by pecuniary gains. It is an esteem that is born in sharp contests and thrives despite conflicting interests. It is an esteem commanded solely by integrity of character and by brains and skill in the honorable performance of professional duty."[15]

So said Chief Justice Hughes. That is the esteem—the friendship—which we of the trial bar feel so strongly for George Boldt. It is the friendship which comes from years of working together on hard causes and through great difficulties, year after year. There is no substitute for it; there is nothing else in life quite like it.

That is why the officers and trustees of the Seattle-King County Bar Association, representing nearly three thousand lawyers of King County, have unanimously voted to honor Judge Boldt on this occasion. Their resolution and their plaque says:

> In Appreciation of His 25 Years
> of Outstanding Service
> on the Federal Bench
> This Award Is Presented to
> The Honorable George H. Boldt

By the Seattle–King County Bar Association
July, 1978

George, I present you this award with the thanks and admiration of all of us. May you have many more years on the bench.
Congratulations!

NOTES

1 William A. Helsell (1924–) was a member of what is now Helsell Fetterman, a Seattle law firm, and was president of the Seattle–King County Bar Association in 1978–79.

2 George Hugo Boldt (1903–84) served as a U.S. District Court judge for the Eastern District of Washington from 1953 until his death in 1984.

3 In the late 1940s, George Boldt practiced with the firm of Metzger, Blair, Gardner & Boldt.

4 *U.S. v. Northern Pacific R.R., & Northwestern Improvement Company,* 142 F. Supp. 679 (1956), aff'd 356 U.S. 1 (1958).

5 *U.S. v. Dave Beck,* 3 AFTR 2d 1364 (W. D. Wash. 1959).

6 *U.S. v. Mickey Cohen,* 297 F.2d 760 (9th Cir., 1962), an appeal from the decision rendered by Judge Boldt.

7 *U.S. v. Carbo,* 357 F.2d 800 (9th Cir., 1966), an appeal from a denial of a motion by Judge Boldt in the Southern District of California.

8 In 1970, Judge Boldt presided in Tacoma over the trial of the "Seattle Seven," a case that grew out of the indictment of SLF members for their conspiracy to plan a riot during a political protest. After several disruptions to the trial and a walkout by the defendants, Judge Boldt declared a mistrial, following which charges were dropped when the defendants agreed not to challenge their contempt citations.

9 *U.S. v. Washington,* 384 F. Supp. 312 (W.D. Wash. 1974), aff'd 520 F.2d 676 (9th Cir. 1975).

10 *Labbee v. Wm. Wrigley, Jr., Co.,* no. 4029, W.D. Wash., filed 1/13/70. In this particular matter, Dwyer, while in private practice, represented a group of mint growers residing in Washington and Oregon in a class action leveled

against major mint oil purchasers. The complaint sought treble damages alleging price fixing, group boycott, and monopolization. The private antitrust case was settled in 1975 on the eve of trial, with the plaintiff's receiving a multimillion dollar cash payment. Detail on the settlement can be found in the *Antitrust & Trade Reg. Rep.* (BNA), no. 719, at A-29 (June 24, 1975).

11 *Wynn Oil Co. v. Percolator Chemical Corp.*, 536 F. 2d 84 (5th Cir., 1976).

12 In 1975, twenty-one private actions concerning alleged antitrust violations in the sugar industry filed in four different districts were transferred by the Judicial Panel on Multidistrict Litigation to the U.S. District Court for Northern California and assigned to Judge Boldt, who had gained experience with the sugar industry in a case filed in his district court in 1972.

13 In 1971, President Nixon created the Cost of Living Council to oversee two parts of the economy: the Price Commission, which controlled price increases, and the Pay Board, which controlled wage increases.

14 The University of Puget Sound Law School was transferred to Seattle University on August 19, 1994, and since that date has operated as Seattle University School of Law.

15 Chief Justice Hughes, "Remarks in Reference to the Late George Wickersham," *Proceedings* 13, American Law Institute (1936).

New Dimensions

June 28, 2001

D EAN HJORTH, DEAN-DESIGNATE KNIGHT, PROFESSOR Jay, Professor Junker, members of the faculty, students and alumni, ladies and gentlemen, and my three oldest grandchildren, Maxwell, Henry, and Sam:

It is a pleasure to be here among so many old friends and fellow citizens who were unable to get tickets to this afternoon's Mariners game. And of course I am deeply honored, all the more so because today's ceremony ranks high on the scale of unexpected events. The gratitude I feel at the creation of this endowed chair is matched only by a strong sense of surprise.[1] While I am surprised, my classmates must be amazed. And my teachers of long ago, who had every right to consider me a phantom, would be astounded. But destiny often brings the improbable, and here we are.

Destiny, in this case, would have gotten nowhere without the dedicated and resourceful efforts of Dean Hjorth, Assistant Dean Dexter

Bailey, Professor Meade Emory, Provost Lee Huntsman, President Richard McCormick, and others at the University of Washington, and without the generosity of those who have donated to this cause. All of them have my heartfelt thanks and the gratitude of all who care about this law school, for it is the school that will benefit.

Their combined efforts, I understand, have produced an endowment of one million dollars. In the American English I grew up speaking, that phrase did not describe a real or understandable amount of money; it was only a kind of hyperbolic superlative, as in, "She has a million-dollar smile" or "You look like a million dollars tonight." Nowadays, having experienced prosperity and inflation, we can picture a seven-figure bank deposit slip, but most of us still would wonder whether a decimal point had been misplaced. So when a friend asked the other day if I had endowed the chair myself, I took it as a financial compliment. I could not take it as a professional compliment, though, because the canons of judicial ethics require that I take no part in fund-raising for an honor of this nature. Not only that, they say that, so long as I continue to hear cases, I should make "reasonable efforts" to avoid learning who has contributed. I have made those efforts, and I remain ignorant. So my thanks, at least for now, must go to donors whose generosity is known to me but whose identities are not.

The dedication of this chair is a vote of confidence in the future, in the new dimensions that make legal education deeper, more searching, and more vitally connected to the outside world than it used to be.

When my classmates and I arrived here in 1949, this was an excellent law school, but it was very different from what we see today. It was easy to get in but hard to get out alive; like fish eggs spawned in the open sea, few of us would escape the dangers all around. The professors taught chiefly by the Socratic method, aiming to transform the mush in our heads into minds capable of legal reasoning. Many students were flunked out in the first and second years, leaving, at the end, a small band of survivors who had bonded as friends. To this day some of my best friends—including my long-time partners Gordon Culp and Murray Guterson—are from that entering class.

Today, the University of Washington School of Law, like other high-quality institutions, is hard to get into—but the student, once admitted, is nurtured toward graduation. The flunk-out rate has plummeted.

Legal education, back then, was strong on case analysis and doctrine, but weak on the big picture—history, comparative law, and professional responsibility—and weak on skills training.

Today the Socratic method lives on and still provides some entertainment, and learning how to think like a lawyer remains vital. But there is a far richer variety of courses and greatly improved training in the skills needed for success: writing, negotiation technique, advocacy, mediation, and so on. The course catalogue reads like a fascinating itinerary through the wide world of the law.

The faculty in our time was composed almost entirely of white males, and the student body was emphatically not diverse: our entering class had three women and one person of color. (That one person is my old friend Jack Tanner, now a U.S. district judge for the Western District of Washington at Tacoma.[2]) Today, the faculty is both distinguished and diverse, and so is the student body: half the students are women and about a fourth are minorities.

Back then the school received only a smattering of gifts; there was no law school foundation and no office of development. Today, private gifts—which are necessary to any state institution that hopes to be great—have lifted this law school to a new level of distinction. We now have twelve professorships and two chairs, and there will be more. Much of the cost of William H. Gates Hall will come from private donations.[3] Fund-raising has become an important part of the school's life and is expertly managed.

There is another new dimension that goes to the heart of legal education, law practice, and, in fact, our entire system of justice. It has to do with the four words that appear over the Supreme Court's entrance: Equal Justice Under Law.

As lawyers and judges we habitually concentrate on the work at hand—the trial in progress, the document to be drafted, the negotiation to be conducted—and we take pride in the skillful and ethical performance of these functions. Most of us are too busy, or think we are, to remember the appalling fact that two-thirds to three-fourths of the legal needs of poor Americans go unmet because legal services are unavailable or unaffordable. That estimate comes from a reliable source—the American Bar Association. Justice for the poor too often bears no resemblance to justice for the rich.

Everyone agrees that this gap should be closed, but how to do it? Of course it isn't a problem just of the legal profession. As a society we should widen the circle of those who enjoy the full benefits of our legal system; for example, by funding legal aid agencies and neighborhood dispute-resolution centers. But unequal justice is of special concern to the bench and bar. We are the stewards and trustees of the legal system; we enjoy a traditional monopoly in dispute resolution; and we have enormous power in American society. The canons of ethics of Washington and many other states urge all members of the bar to donate substantial working time to pro bono services. These are only aspirational statements—they express hopes, not commands—and most lawyers, nationwide, find themselves too busy to make time for such work.

Some do give generously of their time and talent—I have known many such lawyers, including a few real pro bono heroes—and the entire profession, I believe, will improve its performance. In the meantime, a sterling example is being set at the University of Washington School of Law. A few years ago the law students voted to impose on themselves a requirement for graduation that at least sixty hours of public service work be performed. The program has been a tremendous success. Some students work in clinics that afford legal help to immigrants, the unemployed, Social Security applicants, children, and other disadvantaged persons. Others work in public interest law firms or defenders' or prosecutors' offices or judges' chambers. Education is enriched, practical experience is gained, and when they graduate, the new lawyers enter the profession knowing that the ideal of equal justice *can* be brought to life. There could be no more important lesson to take into a new career.

All of this leads to an expression of my great pleasure over Stewart Jay's appointment as first holder of the new chair. I have known and admired Professor Jay since he first came here from the distant East. He is a person who cares passionately about justice, as I have learned in working with him on bench-bar committees and other projects. He is also a brilliant teacher, scholar, writer, and historian. And, I must say, a fine debater—a couple of times, years ago, he and I debated for student audiences the question, Which is better: the adversary system or the inquisitorial system? I can only express my relief that nobody kept score. I congratulate Professor Jay, and I consider it an honor to have my name linked with his in the education of law students.

"Change everything except your loves," said Voltaire. Much has changed in the half century since my classmates and I first entered old Condon Hall.[4] The Cold War, which seemed interminable, has ended; major league baseball has come to Seattle, and gone away, and come again, this time to stay; the Kingdome has risen and stood for two decades and then vanished in a cloud of dust; the law school has changed buildings (for the worse) and soon will change again (for the infinitely better). All of us have been changed by time and circumstance. But I have never changed the two loves I found here. One of them I recognized right away; she is with us today and is probably the only person in the world with the transnational name of Vasiliki Dwyer. The other dawned on me more slowly but has grown and deepened over time. That is the legal profession, with its camaraderie, its challenges, its opportunities for adventure, and its ever renewed invitation to give the best that is in us.

The great poet Theodore Roethke, who taught and wrote on this campus, left us the words that are engraved by a doorway in this build-

ing: "I learn by going where I have to go."[5] So it is with all of us—
we learn by going.

Yet where we go, and how we get there, depends to a great extent
on luck. The Danish nuclear physicist Niels Bohr used to keep a horse-
shoe nailed over the door to his workshop. A visitor asked him,
"Surely you don't believe that thing brings you luck?" "Of course
I don't," said Bohr, "but I understand that it works even if you don't
believe in it." Luck! A mysterious force never to be underestimated.
I have had enough of it for several lifetimes, and today's event is a
crowning example.

No one can wish luck into existence, but we can hope; and my hope
today is that this law school, and all of you, will be as fortunate as I
have been.

NOTES

1 The William L. Dwyer Endowed Chair in Law was dedicated on this
day, with Professor Stewart M. Jay installed as the first holder thereof.

2 Jack Edward Tanner was a United States District Judge for the Western
District of Washington from 1978 until he assumed senior status in 1991.
He died in early 2006.

3 William H. Gates Hall was dedicated on September 12, 2003. It is
named for William H. Gates, who graduated from the UW Law School
in 1950.

4 For more than forty years (1932–74), the University of Washington
School of Law occupied "Old Condon Hall" to which Judge Dwyer referred.
The name Condon honored the School's first dean, John T. Condon, who
served from 1899 to 1926.

5 From Roethke's poem "The Waking," first published in *The Waking:
Poems, 1933–53* (New York: Doubleday, 1953).

Judges and Librarians

WASHINGTON LIBRARY ASSOCIATION CONFERENCE

April 29, 1989

I T IS A GREAT PLEASURE TO SPEAK TODAY TO THE librarians of the State of Washington. I was glad to accept this invitation because my gratitude to libraries goes back a long way—back to the discovery of books at good old Interbay Grade School in Seattle.

Nearly all of you here are too young to remember Interbay. It was located in the hollow between Queen Anne Hill and Magnolia. It was just downwind from the city garbage dump. Interbay had an atmosphere all its own. But it also had books—not many, but enough to bring about a case of love at first sight. I still remember maneuvering with the teacher, at the age of about six, for extra time in the book section.

Later, there were the Queen Anne branch of the Seattle Public Library and the new vistas it opened; the libraries at college and law school; and the libraries in several parts of the world where I have spent many happy hours. And, of course, a very enjoyable attorney-client relationship with the Seattle Public Library a few years ago.

But this affinity with libraries is not just personal. It is also professional. There is a natural bond between libraries and the law—between judges and librarians. Why? Because we are both guardians of books; we are both, you might say, guardians of the word. This kinship shows up most clearly and most dramatically in the ever recurring battles over censorship.

Censorship is probably as old as written language. It may be as old as spoken language. In the long course of history, censorship has been much more prevalent than freedom of expression. It has been imposed on political, religious, and moral grounds. It has flourished in official and unofficial forms.

Among the many whose works have been censored over the centuries have been most of the great writers of ancient Greece and Rome; Martin Luther; Shakespeare, whose plays for a time were available only in a bowdlerized version in parts of this country; Gustav Flaubert, who was prosecuted for having published *Madame Bovary*; and a host of others.

In most times and places censorship has not been limited to the obscene. Often it has not been bounded by law at all. Countless works that were found to be sacrilegious, subversive, or merely offensive, have been suppressed.

But the modern world has seen the birth of a new fundamental right: the right of all persons to speak, publish, and read freely. Beginning with the seventeenth century we can trace the landmarks: in 1644, John Milton's *Areopagitica*; in the eighteenth century, the American Bill of Rights and the French Declaration of the Rights of Man; in the nineteenth, John Stuart Mills' essay "On Liberty."

The right of free expression has been with us, more or less, for only a few hundred years. No country has ever treated it as absolute. Every society, ours included, imposes legal limits on speech under some circumstances. But the right is priceless; it is central to the dignity of man; and it has been hard-won by the sacrifices of men and women who demanded it and defended it.

In the United States we believe that freedom of expression keeps our society open and dynamic. We have in our Constitution the First Amendment, which says: "Congress shall make no law abridging the freedom of speech or of the press . . . " The amendment applies to the federal government and to the states. It guarantees, among other things, libraries free of censorship.

We know also that freedom of expression enjoys, at any given time, only a mixed popularity. That is true because it necessarily permits the publication of works that cause offense; works that are of dubious value; works that we feel sure have only a negative effect.

If you and I were to take a stroll through the supermarket newsstands of this city, we would have no trouble at all in picking out hundreds of books, magazines, and newspapers that are fit only for the trash can. But we certainly don't want anyone else to make the selection—just you and I. And after a little exposure to my old-fashioned taste, you probably would decide to dispense with my help and do the whole job yourself.

We don't try to weed the field of publications because no one is wise enough to be the gardener. American history—like world history—proves it. Valuable books, even great books, have been banned or bowdlerized in America as elsewhere.

In 1885 the Board of Trustees of the Concord, Massachusetts, public library voted to exclude a book from the shelves. One trustee noted that the book "deals with a series of adventures of a very low grade of morality, it is couched in the language of a rough dialect, and all through its pages there is a systematic use of bad grammar. . . . The book is flippant and irreverent. . . . It is trash of the veriest sort." The banned book was Mark Twain's classic *Huckleberry Finn*. Twain, on hearing the news from Concord, said it would increase his sales by 25,000 copies.

Walt Whitman's *Leaves of Grass* was once banned in Boston. And we have seen the suppression of works by James Joyce, Henry Miller, Theodore Dreiser, Bernard Malamud, Kurt Vonnegut, and many others—even of *Huckleberry Finn,* again, although this time for different reasons.

Seattle, like every other city, has had its battles over censorship. Some of these have involved motion pictures. For many years, the City Council empowered a group called the Board of Theater Supervisors to preview films and make "recommendations" that they not be shown or that scenes be cut. The city had the power to license businesses, and the exhibitors usually went along with the recommendations. Films that could not legally be suppressed—even some films that were good—fell victim, in whole or in part, to this method of semi-official censorship. Finally, the state Supreme Court held the system unconstitutional. This happened not so long ago—the year was 1966.

There have also been local battles over written and graphic publications. In one of them the proprietor and clerk of the Id Bookstore in the University District of Seattle were prosecuted for having two items on sale in the store. One was the "Kama Sutra Calendar," which had photographs of semi-abstract metallic sculptures based on scenes from the *Kama Sutra;*[1] the other was a vulgar and outspoken, but legally protected, magazine with the uninviting title of *Entrails.* The defendants were tried in Superior Court and found not guilty. The year was 1968.

The most recent instance of attempted censorship took place this year. It involved a book called *Satanic Verses* by Salman Rushdie. The head of a certain government in the Middle East uttered death threats against anyone who took part in distributing the book. A wave of withdrawals followed in the United States and elsewhere. But not at the Seattle Public Library. Elizabeth Stroup, the librarian, said: "This library subscribes to freedom to read ... if any terrorists come, I hope they ask for Liz."[2]

A proud moment for the libraries of our state—and a reminder of what Elmer Davis said: "This will remain the land of the free only so long as it is the home of the brave."[3]

When it comes to censorship, the role of judges complements the role of librarians. Our duty is to apply the law faithfully. That includes safeguarding the constitutional liberty that is basic in our law. Without the courts—as without the libraries—that freedom would not survive.

Censorship battles of the past give us a treasury of war stories, and provide the most obvious examples of how law and libraries relate to each other. But they also reflect a broader and more profound connection between judges and librarians. Both professions are guardians of the word in a larger sense.

"In the beginning was the word," says the Gospel according to St. John. And, fifteen centuries later, Montaigne wrote: "We are not men, nor have any tie upon one another, but by our word . . . " (Nowadays, of course, Montaigne would substitute "human" for "men.")

And it is true that our use of language is what distinguishes us from all other creatures and lifts us to whatever heights we can attain. The most enduring landmarks of our species are collections of words: the Bible, the works of Shakespeare, the American Constitution and Bill of Rights, the Universal Declaration of Human Rights, to name a few.

Words form the compacts by which we live. And in this culture of words, where would our civilization be—where would we be— without librarians? It is they who have preserved what we have, not just against censors but against other adversaries: decay, fire, accidental loss, and carelessness.

What has been lost over the centuries is beyond reckoning: uncounted works of literature, history, science, poetry, and correspondence.

To take one example, Sophocles lived to be ninety in ancient Greece. He was one of the greatest playwrights who ever lived. We know that he wrote more than a hundred plays. Seven have survived—among them the immortal classics *Oedipus Rex* and *Electra*.[4] More than ninety of his plays have been lost—including what masterpieces we will never know.

Everything Sophocles wrote could have been lost. Seven plays were saved, apparently, in a schoolmaster's selection kept in the ancient library at Alexandria, Egypt. That library lasted for five centuries, until the late third century, A.D.

We do not know what was lost when the library at Alexandria was destroyed. We do know that much of what was saved, then and later, was saved by librarians. Ancient Greek works were preserved at Constantinople during the European Dark Ages; Latin texts were saved by Charlemagne's scholars. By the skin of our teeth we emerged from the Dark Ages into the Middle Ages, the Renaissance, and the modern world with part of the heritage of ancient Greece and Rome—thanks to librarians.

And so it has been through history.

Libraries represent our collective memory. Without it—without them—we would be lost. We would lose our train of thought; our continuity; our hold on the great network of words that binds us to our forebears and to each other.

The judges' work is equally married to words and the integrity of words. Law is a system of rights; of commands; of officially shared values; and of procedures meant to provide fairness to all. "The life of the law has not been logic; it has been experience," said Oliver Wendell Holmes.[5] That is true, but the experience is made up of words; lived through words; remembered through words; and passed on through words, in the law libraries, to future generations.

Law only works if judges and juries are true to its language; if the words are clear; and if the words keep their integrity. Many countries have high-sounding constitutions, but only a few have real liberty.

George Orwell showed us brilliantly how freedom depends on the integrity of language. If words are debased, the liberties that are sustained by words are in peril. And the more our public life moves away from words—the more it depends on non-verbal symbols and pictures—the more our liberties are at risk.

In the late twentieth century, there is a disturbing trend toward the debasement of language, as well as toward a reliance on symbols and catch phrases.

The choice is ours to make. We can choose to keep books in their prominent place. We can use language with the respect it deserves as mankind's greatest single achievement.

If we do these things we will honor the past and have hope for the future. And we will have hope for our children. The children, after all, depend on your profession and mine—on how well and how faithfully we do our work.

The Seattle poet David Wagoner must have given a talk to a meeting of librarians some years ago. He has a fine poem called "After the Speech to the Librarians."[6] It tells how he takes a walk in the country, feeling he should have done better with the speech, and comes to a field. In the field are horses, a marsh hawk, and some small birds called water pipits. The poem has a word in it, "whickering," which many of us city people don't recognize right away. A whicker to a horse is the same as a whinny. This is how the poem ends:

> When I wasn't looking, the hawk flew suddenly,
> Skimming the field, effortlessly graceful, tilting
> And scanning at low-level: he stops
> Dead without slowing down, swivels
> And drops into the grass, flashing white
> And tawny, rises at full speed carrying nothing
> And goes on soaring, slanting downhill
> No higher than my head, making his sharp outcry.
> The water pipits answer, thin as fence-wire.
> Isn't it wonderful not being dead yet?
> Their breasts all hold the same air
> As his and the softly whickering unsaddled horses'
> And mine and the Librarians'
> With which we all might sing for the children.

1 The title of an ancient Sanskrit treatise on the art of love and sexual techniques.

2 Elizabeth ("Liz") Stroup was Seattle City Librarian from 1988 to 1996.

3 From Elmer Davis' book, *But We Were Born Free* (Indianapolis: Bobbs-Merrill [1954]). Davis (1890–1958) was a news broadcaster and writer and director of the U.S. Office of War Information during World War II.

4 Only seven of Sophocles' tragedies survive in their entirety. The two mentioned, written in the fifth century B.C., are in that group.

5 Holmes, *The Common Law* (Boston: Little, Brown, 1881), p. 1.

6 David Wagoner, *Through the Forest: New and Selected Poems, 1977–1987* (New York: Atlantic Monthly Press, 1987).

The Declaration of the Rights of Man—
200 Years Later

SEATTLE-NANTES SISTER CITY ASSOCIATION

October 1, 1989

IT IS A GREAT PLEASURE TO APPEAR BEFORE THIS society devoted to friendship between the United States and France and to speak on one of the world's most important subjects— liberty.

In 1789, early in the French Revolution, there appeared one of the great documents of history. It was called the Declaration of the Rights of Man and of the Citizen.[1] It proclaimed to the world the ideas behind the revolution that toppled the old regime and changed the course of history.

Countless men and women were inspired by it. William Wordsworth was moved by the Declaration and its philosophy to write the famous lines:

> Bliss was it in that dawn to be alive,
> But to be young was very heaven![2]

The historian Lord Acton later captured both the flaws and the influence of the Declaration when he called it "a single confused page . . . that outweighed libraries and was stronger than all the armies of Napoleon."[3]

Two hundred years have gone by. We are more experienced, if not wiser, and it is fitting that we now take stock of this Declaration, see what it has meant to the world, and think about what the future may hold for it and for us.

The Declaration was a founding document of liberty—of "human rights," to use today's term. Human rights are comparatively new on the world scene. Only of late, as history goes, have they been clearly defined and systematically afforded by governments. There were landmarks, of course, before the French Revolution. There was Magna Carta, in 1215 A.D. There was the English Bill of Rights in 1689— three hundred years ago—a priceless document but mainly provincial, mainly for England.

There were the bills of rights of several American colonies. There was the American Declaration of Independence of 1776, saying it was "self-evident"—a lot of time can be saved if something is announced as self-evident—that "all men are created equal [and are] endowed by their creator with certain inalienable rights." These American examples were inspiring, but they came from a new, remote, and thinly populated place.

France, on the other hand, in 1789 was a great power, the most populous country in Europe, with 26 million people. It had a proud history and a civilizing mission. Its Declaration two hundred years ago was by no means provincial. This was a universal proclamation; an insight into the nature of mankind; a trumpeting of the rights of all men, everywhere. It sounded throughout Europe, and it echoes throughout the world today.

In a sense the Declaration was a French-American production. The main author of the first draft was Lafayette, George Washington's unofficially adopted son. Drafts were reviewed by Thomas Jefferson, then in Paris as the American legate. Among the sources drawn upon were the constitutions of Virginia and New Hampshire.

There were, of course, French sources: Montesquieu, whose doctrine of the separation of powers also shaped the American Constitution of 1787; the Encyclopedists and their belief in natural rights (with credit to John Locke); Voltaire, who insisted that the individual be safeguarded against arbitrary police or judicial action; Rousseau, with his theory of the general will"; and the Physiocrats, who argued for the sanctity of private property.

The Declaration was adopted by the Constituent Assembly on August 4, 1789. Louis XVI was still king of France. He accepted it on October 5, 1789—two hundred years ago this week—during riots that forced him the next day to leave Versailles for Paris. The Declaration became a preamble to the French Constitution adopted in 1791. Some version of it has appeared in every French constitution since then.

The original 1789 version had seventeen articles. These are the highlights:

It begins: "All men are born and remain free"—an echo of Rousseau's unforgettable opening sentence, "Man was born free, and everywhere is in chains."[4]

It continues: ". . . and have equal rights. Social distinctions are unjustifiable except insofar as they may serve the common good." Farewell, hereditary nobility.

It goes on to list the "inalienable rights of man—liberty, private property, the inviolability of the person, and the right to resist oppression." Note that the practical French listed "private property" as a basic right. Thirteen years earlier, similar language had been removed from an early draft of our Declaration of Independence and was replaced by the vaguer and more idealistic "pursuit of happiness."

Liberty, says the French Declaration, means the right to do anything which does not harm others. It says that "law is the overt expression of the general will." This idea, from Rousseau, has been a mixed blessing. In our century, it has been seized upon, perversely, to justify fascism.

The document goes on to say that "all are equal before the law, [and] all are equally eligible, in accordance with their abilities, for all public offices and positions." And: "No man can be . . . arrested or held . . . except for offenses legally defined." This, of course, is part of what we call due process of law. The cautious French have added: ". . . but if a citizen is summoned or arrested in due legal form it is his duty to obey instantly"—what you might call the "don't mess with the gendarmes" provision.

The Declaration prohibits ex post facto crimes and all legal penalties except those that are "obviously necessary." It says that everyone is presumed innocent, and prohibits unnecessary force in arrests or detentions. "No one must suffer for his opinions, even for religious opinions"—this is a counterpart of our First Amendment, but again the French have added a qualifier—"provided that his advocacy of them does not endanger public order."

"Free communication of thought and opinion is one of the most valuable rights of man; thus, every citizen may speak, write, and print his views freely." Then, again, a qualifier: "provided only that he accepts the bounds of this freedom established by law." Our First Amendment is more sweeping. It says simply: "Congress shall make no law abridging the freedom of speech or of the press."

"A society in which rights are not guaranteed, and in which there is no separation of powers, has no constitution." This comes from Montesquieu.[5]

Private property is declared to be "sacred and inviolable."

By our lights today, the Declaration has some major omissions. Perhaps the most glaring is that it speaks only about "man," not "woman." In 1790, a Parisian actress by the name of Olympe de Gouges fought back by publishing a Declaration of the Rights of Women.[6] It got nowhere at the time, but its author might be pleased by a visit to a western democracy today.

In practice the Declaration was followed by measures limiting the right to vote to French males over twenty-five who had an established domicile for one year, were not domestic servants or dependents, and paid the equivalent of three days' labor in taxes (cutting out millions of male French citizens); by the retention of slavery in the colonies; by the Terror in which perhaps 17,000 citizens were executed; and by the wars and repressions of the later French Revolution.

Nevertheless, the Declaration of the Rights of Man brought a new dimension of hope and freedom to the world. Through the nineteenth and early twentieth centuries human rights struggle went on. There have been gains and losses. The most famous case in France was that of Captain Alfred Dreyfus, falsely accused and imprisoned for treason but vindicated in the end.

Then came World War I, the seminal modern catastrophe. And after that war, the darkest hours for liberty in the modern era. Human rights were crushed by fascist regimes in Germany and Italy and by a communist regime in Russia. The world saw not just restrictions on speech and dissent, but mass murder.

World War II came, and it was fought, more than any other war in history, in the name of human rights. After the Allies won, the world was horrified by what had happened, above all, by the genocide practiced by the Nazis. The United Nations was formed in the hope of achieving international peace and justice. And in 1948, its members adopted, without a dissenting vote, this century's great human rights document—the Universal Declaration of Human Rights.[7]

The contributions of France, England, and the United States were vital to this historic achievement. Among the chief authors were Eleanor Roosevelt of the United States and René Cassin of France.

The Universal Declaration placed human rights in the sphere of international law for the first time. International law had always been concerned with relations between states. Now it looked to the rights of every person against the encroachments of his or her own government. Thus began, four decades ago, an international human rights movement that flourishes today.

The Universal Declaration begins with Rousseau updated: "All human beings are born free and equal in dignity and rights."

It provides that everyone is entitled to all the rights and freedoms it sets forth—without distinction as to race, color, sex, religion, political or other opinion, or origin.

It guarantees all the basic rights: religion, thought and speech, access to the media, assembly, privacy, travel across boundaries, and free choice of place of residence.

It declares the rights to marry and establish a family; to own property; to choose employment freely; and to take part in government.

It proclaims freedom from arbitrary arrest, cruel or inhuman punishment, and ex post facto crimes. It requires fair public trials, an independent judiciary, and the presumption of innocence.

It prohibits torture and slavery, and it proclaims a number of social rights: the rights to work, to equal pay for equal work, to just remuneration, to rest and leisure, to free education, and to an adequate standard of living.

And it provides that everyone is entitled to a social and international order in which these rights and freedoms can be fully realized.

Four decades have gone by. What have the results been?

We read every week of human rights violations, even atrocities: the repression by the Chinese government of student protestors, with jail sentences and even the death penalty; the persecution of dissenters in many countries; religious oppression; torture by the police and by the military; the work of "death squads" clandestinely allied with governments. It is not a rosy picture. But clearly we are aware today, more than we ever have been, of human rights on a worldwide scale.

Now, what of the future? Before revealing what the future holds, I must point out that there are at least three kinds of what we call "human rights."

The first is civil liberties: speech, religion, assembly, due process of law, freedom from race or sex discrimination, the right to be free of torture or enslavement, and so on. These are best suited to the rule of law and are the easiest to measure.

The second category is social rights: the right to a job, to adequate nutrition, housing, education, and the like. These are mushier in concept and are necessarily relative from one country to another.

The third category might be called self-determination rights. Charles DeGaulle, visiting from France, shouted to a crowd in Quebec: "Vive le Quebec libre!"[8] What did he mean? Quebec was already part of a free country, Canada. DeGaulle was not complaining about civil liberties. By "libre" he meant free of the domination of anglophones. Freedom in this sense means freedom from domination by others who are seen as foreign or as usurpers. This category of human rights is so murky as to be almost totally unsuited to law.

All three categories go by the names of "freedom" and "liberty." They have sometimes been treated indiscriminately, as if they were the same; some of the United Nations documents treat them that way. They are not the same, although civil liberties tend to make the other two possible.

Civil liberties are at the heart of human rights, and in assessing where we are today and where we are going, it is civil liberties I will be talking about.

There is plenty of reason to hope—more, perhaps, than ever before. For the first time, we have a worldwide human rights movement. The concept of every person having internationally recognized legal rights has been well described as mankind's first universal ideology.

Amid the reports of violations and atrocities, the human rights movement has been steadily and quietly growing. Several treaties sponsored by the United Nations to implement the Universal Declaration of Human Rights have been adopted by many countries. The most basic are the International Covenant on Civil and Political Rights and the International Covenant on Economic, Social, and Cultural Rights. These embody the provisions of the Universal Declaration in legally binding treaties. About ninety countries, including the western European democracies, have ratified them.

There is also a growing acceptance of the UN–sponsored treaties on genocide, torture, slavery, the rights of women, and racism. As to several of these, it is remarkable that the Soviet Union agreed earlier this year to accept binding arbitration by the World Court.

Regional human rights treaties and courts have also grown in importance. The prime example is found in western Europe, where the European Convention for the Protection of Human Rights and its implementing agencies—a commission and the European Court of Human Rights—have brought an important body of law into existence.

We have seen also in four decades the rise of vigorous private groups that advocate and demand international protection for human rights. The groups include Amnesty International, the International Commission of Jurists, and the various Helsinki watch committees. These private groups are making a difference. They have changed the behavior of governments in many cases. They proceed largely through publicity and public demands for justice under law.

The trend is not limited to single-purpose groups. The American Bar Association, for example, has a number of governing goals. In 1983, a new one was added: "to advance the rule of law in the world." The A.B.A. president last winter said: "To seek international cooperation is no longer optional; it is essential to survival." And he proposed an A.B.A. human rights agenda for the balance of this century.

What has emerged over forty years is an expanding network of domestic law and international treaties, governmental agencies, and private advocacy groups devoted to the protection of human rights. These reflect the beliefs of countless individual people. We see now a worldwide demand for human rights—the same demand that fired the French Declaration and the American Bill of Rights two centuries ago. We see it today in the Soviet Union, in eastern Europe, and in China; we've seen the recent victories of this popular demand in Spain, Portugal, Greece, and parts of Latin America.

Can these voices be stilled?

If prosperity spreads and modern communications continue to grow, it will become increasingly difficult to still them. Jacques Delors, president of the European Commission in Brussels, said this year: "What has sparked the lightning flash of freedom through the communist countries, if not rock music and American movies?" Let's hope it's something less cacophonous than rock music. But the fact is that global electronic communication helps.

There are other necessary conditions to the health of human rights. Foremost is peace. War always diminishes liberty. Even Abraham Lincoln suspended the writ of habeas corpus in wartime. The current "drug war," while not strictly speaking a war, exerts pressure on the rule of law.

Another condition is the avoidance of overpopulation. Human rights would have a hard time in a sardine-can society. And another is preservation of the physical world—environmental preservation. Through human rights we save ourselves from ourselves. We must also save the planet from ourselves, and these two necessities are linked.

It is time to close. As Voltaire said, "The surest way of being a bore is to tell everything." Will we arrive at the millennium, a golden moment when human rights are fully realized for every man, woman, and child on earth?

Definitely not.

We may even fail disastrously, if we are inept enough. But the quest for the liberties of the great eighteenth-century declarations is one of our highest callings, and if we give it the best that is in us, we can draw much closer to a world in which everyone is truly "born free."

1 The Declaration of the Rights of Man and the Citizen was adopted by the Constituent Assembly in 1789 and embodied in the French Constitution of 1791 as a preamble.

2 William Wordsworth (1770–1850), *The Prelude*, Book 11, ll. 108–9.

3 The quote from Lord Acton (John Emerich Edward Dalberg Acton) is discussed in Hersch Lauterpacht, *International Law and Human Rights* (1950), p. 126.

4 For Rousseau's quotations, see *The Social Contract, and Discourses*, trans. G. D. H. Cole (New York: Dutton, 1950; rev. ed., 1973), pp. 163, 165.

5 Quoted in Louis Henkin, "Elements of Constitutionalism," in *The Review: The International Commission of Jurists* (1998), pp. 1023, 1025.

6 Olympe de Gouges, a butcher's daughter, proved to be one of the most outspoken and articulate women revolutionaries in France. In 1791, as a playwright of some note, she challenged the inferior status of women presumed by the Declaration of the Rights of Man by writing and publishing *The Declaration of the Rights of Woman and the Citizen.*

7 The Universal Declaration of Human Rights was adopted by the United Nations General Assembly on December 10, 1948 (Gen. Ass. Resolution 217A [III]).

8 DeGaulle's statement on July 24, 1967, was part of Canada's Quiet Revolution of the mid-1960s.

Optimism for Lawyers

ANNUAL BANQUET, THE ORDER OF THE COIF

UNIVERSITY OF WASHINGTON SCHOOL OF LAW

July 23, 1992

D EAN LOH, MEMBERS OF THE FACULTY, HONORED guests, ladies and gentlemen. I feel lucky to be here tonight and especially lucky to be introduced by Jack Sullivan.[1] I have known Professor Sullivan for a long time. He was, and is, an exemplary trial lawyer. For twelve years he has run the trial advocacy program at the University of Washington School of Law. He has made it into one of the finest such programs in the country. No one has ever done more for trial advocacy in the Northwest than Jack Sullivan. He is retiring this year, and we are all greatly in his debt.

My heartfelt thanks to the faculty for selecting me for the Order of the Coif award. I am greatly honored. To those of the class of 1952 who made Order of the Coif the hard way, and who might think this award is unjust, I can only point out that you have had a handsome certificate on your wall for forty years in a spot where I have had to make do with an old photograph of a fishing trip.

And to the new members of the Order of the Coif, who have just graduated: Congratulations, and welcome to our great profession.

"Optimism for lawyers" is what I'd like to talk to you about.

I am aware that Ambrose Bierce, in *The Devil's Dictionary*, defined optimism as the "belief that everything is beautiful, including what is ugly—everything good, especially the bad—and everything right that is wrong."[2] He called it "an intellectual disorder, yielding to no treatment but death."

I am also aware of milder but equally dismissive views of optimism. It has been said that "an optimist is one who believes that this is the best of all possible worlds; a pessimist is one who is afraid the optimist is right."

I like optimism better than that. For one thing, it is essential to our calling as lawyers. The basic assumption of law is that people will live by the rules. In other words, that they will be civilized. An optimistic assumption. The basic assumptions of democracy are that people are capable of governing themselves, and that the conditions of freedom—especially freedom of speech and of the press—give them the means of doing so. These beliefs also are optimistic.

Our free institutions are beautifully designed but they must be operated capably, honestly, and with confidence. The art historian Kenneth Clark wrote: "It is lack of confidence, more than anything else, that kills a civilization. We can destroy ourselves by cynicism and disillusion, just as effectively as by bombs."[3]

So optimism has its uses. But it must not be feckless; it must be based on knowledge and understanding.

In our own field, the basic assumptions are that the law is a high calling; that it is the profession most vitally linked to justice, self—government, and the improvement of the human condition; that it works; and that it is worth devoting one's life to. Without those assumptions the practice of law can become drudgery littered with time slips and spoiled weekends. But with them, there is no better life than a life in the law.

I also decided to talk about optimism because we have had so much bad news for so long—to the point where many thoughtful people believe the world is doomed, or at least mankind is doomed, and certainly democracy is doomed.

The question is: Can optimism be justified today? A look around us might not be instantly encouraging. Let's take a quick survey of the bad news:

In the world at large, we have overpopulation, pollution of the air and water, depletion of resources, and severe and growing damage to natural systems. These trends call into question the future of life on earth, and they have already ruined the quality of life in many places.

A global warming trend, to which we contribute, foretells a rising of the seas and eventual submersion of coastal cities.

Gaps in the ozone layer, caused by our excesses here below, are making sunshine dangerous.

Poverty blights the lives of billions.

Famine still takes the lives of children.

War breaks out again and again.

An enormous number of atomic warheads exist in the world, and the technology of making them becomes ever more accessible.

Ethnic and religious hatreds flourish.

Basic liberties—even so basic a one as the right to be free of torture—are denied in many parts of the world.

In the United States we still have an unresolved problem of race relations, one hundred and fifty years after Alexis de Tocqueville wrote that race war "is a nightmare constantly haunting the American imagination,"[4] one hundred and twenty-seven years after the Civil War, and nearly forty years after *Brown v. Board of Education*,[5] we have tensions between believers in one ideology or another; decaying inner cities containing what has come to be called an "underclass" of under-educated and largely unemployed people; a public school system heavily damaged by lack of resources and low morale; millions of citizens whose lives are so empty that they resort to the use of illegal narcotic drugs; and a mammoth national debt run up by years of deficit spending. Some say the American dream is over.

In our own field, we see courts overloaded to the point where in some major cities civil cases must languish for five or six years before trial, or may never get to trial at all; a civil litigation system grown so expensive that most people cannot afford to use it; criminal sentencing laws that demand ever increasing use of imprisonment, leading to predictable over-crowding of the prisons and other unwanted consequences; and, among some lawyers, a loss of civility and pride and a decline into over-contentiousness and greed, to the detriment of the values that have made our profession great.

Well, I can see that this list has had a depressing effect on the room, but we must recognize that it is not complete. It does give a sampling, though, of the difficulties that face us. And I trust it is enough to show that I am not Voltaire's Dr. Pangloss.[6] I do not believe that all is well.

But I *do* believe that we can climb out of the pit we have dug ourselves into. In a world where a Japanese-backed group can buy the Seattle Mariners, and win the approval of the major league baseball owners, anything good can happen.

Let's look at today's challenges in light of what we have achieved in the past and what we can achieve in the future.

It is true that the world is threatened with physical ruin because of mankind's excesses, and that to avoid this will take a tremendous feat of skill, purpose, and collective determination.

But we are the species that invented language. We invented agriculture. We invented towns, cities, and civilization.

The present crisis has come on very fast. The Industrial Age itself is little more than the blink of an eye in the long course of history.

We have had very little time to react—and we are reacting. The

Rio de Janeiro conference just ended showed a world-wide consensus that a solution must be found.[7] It even showed a degree of willingness to pay for it.

Imaginative steps are in the works, such as exchanging third-world debt for tropical forest preservation. Local efforts will be vital. One of the best anywhere has succeeded right here—the cleanup of Lake Washington by Metro.[8]

We have at our command the profound and marvelous insights of twentieth-century science.

We have gotten rid of smallpox, polio, and bubonic plague.

We have set foot on the moon and sent ourselves messages from Mars.

We can do what has to be done to save the earth—if we choose to.

It is true that poverty and famine are still with us. But it is also true that there is a green revolution; that greatly increased agricultural production, without harmful side-effects, can be achieved; that population control has become a reality in some parts of the world; and that education and enlightened economics have yet to be tried in other parts.

We can eradicate poverty and famine—if we choose to.

It is true that war is still with us. But it is also true that, despite the tens of thousands of atomic weapons in the world, we have gone through forty-seven years without a single one being used in battle. The main adversaries have now reached agreements for partial disarmament, and that trend can spread. We have recently seen a remarkable use of international law, under United Nations auspices, in responding to one nation's attack upon another. Whatever one may believe about the causes or the outcome of the Iraq/Kuwait episode, the important fact for law is that the responding operation was mounted in the name of international law. A valuable precedent has been created. And the recognition that war must end is growing.

It is true that ethnic and religious hatred still exists. But it is much less prevalent than it has been through most of history. Take, as an example, Western Europe. For centuries, its nations fought bitter wars, including the two most catastrophic wars to date. Today they will tell you in France, "C'est tout fini, ca"—it's all over. Hatred between French and Germans and others in Western Europe has virtually disappeared. An economic union is nearly complete despite some recent bumps in the road. Peace and prosperity bless the landscape—demonstrating that we can put war and hatred behind us, if we choose to.

It is true that basic liberties are denied in many countries. But it is also true that the international human rights movement since 1945 has been one of the quietest but most important advances in history. The Universal Declaration of Human Rights, signed in 1948, is one of the greatest of all documents, and it is still comparatively new. Year by year, international human rights law gains strength, and today governments everywhere—even the most oppressive—feel its force and respond to one degree or another. Communism has collapsed nearly everywhere after seven decades of disastrous experiment. The resulting gain for human rights is immeasurable—and if we were not so preoccupied with other things we would still be dancing in the streets about it.

We can extend and strengthen freedom—if we choose to.

In the United States it is true that we still have racial conflict and bias, to our shame, and that we have tensions between ideological opponents (especially where strong religious beliefs are involved).

Does this mean the American dream is over? I don't think so. Mutual respect and tolerance are gained over time. We are still getting there.

Think where we have come from:

Three hundred years ago, in the New England colonies, religious dissenters were not only persecuted but subjected to punishments such as having a hole bored in the tongue that had uttered the offending words.

A hundred and fifty years ago, slavery was still flourishing.

A hundred years ago we had flagrant exploitation of Chinese immigrant workers.

Very recently, we had segregated public schools and other public facilities in the South.

Think how new the enforcement of the civil rights laws is. Think how recent are the successes of organizations like the National Conference of Christians and Jews. We are having growing pains—but we can achieve racial and ethnic diversity, with full mutual respect, if we choose to.

As for the rest of the problems on the U.S. domestic list—decaying inner cities, a large population of undereducated and unemployed, the public schools, the drug problem, the national debt—in the scale of history, these are like the mouse frightening the elephant.

Think what the Germans and Japanese have achieved since their cities lay in rubble in 1945.

Think of the challenges that face other nations today—Peru and Ethiopia, Poland and Russia, for example.

Think of what we ourselves have overcome in the past. Today's problems in the United States become trifling in comparison.

We are the world's richest and most powerful nation, with superb democratic institutions given to us by our forebears. Are we now so weak in the head and heart that we cannot pay our debts and educate our children? I don't think so.

Our people have a pent-up need to work for the common good. It shows in charitable contributions—more than 122 billion dollars in 1990, 90 percent of it from individuals, three times the 1955 amount in constant dollars. It shows in volunteer work, a tremendous force in the United States.

There is a hunger in the country to be told the truth. The law of supply and demand that operates in public life suggests the demand will be filled (at least in part).

We can do what needs to be done—if we choose to. In the legal profession, the adverse trends that I mentioned are real. But it is also true that through law in this country we have gotten rid of slavery, child labor (for the most part), the legalized subjugation of women, sweat shops, officially sanctioned racial discrimination, and a host of other evils. Our Bill of Rights has flourished and grown. Today there are more idealistic lawyers than ever. Pro bono—meaning real and substantial free work for deserving people and causes—is becoming the norm. A grass-roots movement for renewed ethics and civility is gaining strength.

And just in the past generation, the legal profession has opened itself to women and minorities. In our entering class of 1949, as I remember, there were three women and one black person. Today, the University of Washington Law School student body has 47 percent women and 30 percent members of minorities; in the entering 1992 class, about 38 percent will be members of minority groups. This reflects one of the happiest changes in the history of American law.

With the help of lawyers, teachers, and judges, progress is being made in reforming civil litigation to make it affordable, swift, and fair.

We can preserve and enhance the law and the legal profession— if we choose to.

The tasks before us are not easy and some of them will be of monumental difficulty.

But we will do well to remember the position Winston Churchill was in 1940. France had fallen to the Nazis, Poland and Czechoslovakia and the Low Countries had been overrun, England was on the brink of defeat and occupation. At that moment, which many saw as utterly hopeless, Great Britain finally made Churchill its prime minister. He was sixty-five years old. The burden of saving his country— indeed, the Western World—was on his shoulders. He wrote later in his memoirs:

> As I went to bed at about 3:00 a.m. I was conscious of a profound sense of relief. At last I had the authority to give directions over the whole scene. I felt as if I were walking with

destiny, and that all my past life had been but a preparation
for this hour and for this trial. . . . I thought I knew a good deal
about it all, and I was sure I should not fail. Therefore, although
impatient for the morning, I slept soundly and had no need for
cheering dreams. Facts are better than dreams.[9]

Now, half a century later, the enemies are not simply villains making war, but the subtler menaces that have come with the Industrial
Age, with rampant materialism and overpopulation, with loss of
morale and of a sense of community.

Against these more insidious dangers, can we summon up, as
Churchill did, the necessary fervor, energy, dedication, generosity, and
shared purpose?

We can if we choose to. The real question is: What are we waiting
for?

It has been a pleasure to meet with you. As a new "sergeant at
law" of the Order of the Coif, I am reminded of my years in the Army
long ago. I started as a private and wound up as a first lieutenant. The
men and women I served with back then would not be surprised to
learn that tonight I have been busted back to sergeant.

Thank you.

NOTES

1 Wallace D. Loh was on the faculty of the University of Washington
School of Law from 1974 to 1995; he served as dean from 1990 to 1995.
John J. (Jack) Sullivan taught at the University of Washington School
of Law from 1979 to 1991. He directed the Law School's Trial Advocacy
Program.

2 Ambrose Bierce (1842–1914), *The Devil's Dictionary* (World Publishing Co., 1911).

3 Clark, *Civilisation: A Personal View* (Harper and Row, 1969), p. 347.

4 The exact quote is: "is a danger which . . . perpetually haunts the

imagination of the Americans." Alexis de Tocqueville, *Democracy in America* (London, 1889), vol. 1, p. 382.

5 *Brown v. Board of Education*, 347 U.S. 483 (1954)

6 In Voltaire's philosophical novel, *Candide* (originally published in 1759), the protagonist, Candide, ultimately rejects the philosophy of Dr. Pangloss who maintains that "all is for the best in this best of all possible worlds."

7 The Rio Declaration on Environment and Development was adopted by more than 178 governments at the United Nations Conference on Environment and Development (UNCED) held in Rio de Janerio, June 3–14, 1992.

8 The Municipality of Metropolitan Seattle (Metro) was approved by voters on September 9, 1958. On October 2, 1958, Metro Council was formed for the purpose of cleaning up Lake Washington, because more than a dozen cities and towns in King County discharged some 20 million gallons of inadequately treated sewage into Lake Washington each day.

9 Winston Churchill, *The Gathering Storm* (Boston: Houghton Mifflin, 1948).

The Practical Value of Ethics

THE FEDERAL BAR ASSOCIATION OF THE
WESTERN DISTRICT OF WASHINGTON

December 8, 1993

W E ALL KNOW THERE HAS BEEN A DECLINE IN civility and courtesy and dedication to ethics in the practice of law over the past several years. The rule of thumb is that the bigger the city, the worse the problem.

It doesn't have to be that way.

When I was about to become a judge, after thirty years at the trial bar, I had a talk with a retired judge, one of the finest ever to serve around here. "What is most important in doing the job?" I asked him. He quoted an old adage: "A judge should be a gentleman—and if he knows a little law, that's all right too."

The saying needs to be reworded for today's gender-diverse bench, but there is still much truth in it. With a practicing lawyer it's not so simple, but we do have an ancient and honorable tradition. It calls upon us to, in Shakespeare's words, "Do as adversaries do in law— strive mightily, but eat and drink as friends."[1]

The message I give you today is that there is great practical value in courtesy, collegiality, and ethical behavior. These habits are not just consistent with success; they promote success.

We all know what I will call the Motherhood Reason for courtesy and collegiality. It is expressed in the guidelines of professional courtesy adopted by this county's bar association:

> A lawyer owes, to the judiciary and to opposing counsel, a duty of courtesy and cooperation, the observance of which is necessary for the efficient administration of our system of justice and the respect of the public it serves.

This is true and valid. We *do* owe this duty to the court system and the public. And like motherhood, it is hard to argue against. But I will not be talking about it today.

There is a second reason, which I will call the Mirror Reason. When we look into the mirror in the morning, do we want to see a fanatic? The face of a ruthless extremist in the cause of undue advantage and deception? The portrait of Dorian Gray that's been up in the attic all these years? No. Recognizing that we all make our own faces after a certain age, we would rather see Atticus Finch—kindly, wise Gregory Peck—or young and wise Portia.

I will not be talking about the Mirror Reason today.

There is a third reason which I will call the Mundane Reason. It is not so widely recognized, and never the subject of Fourth of July speeches.

It comes to this: civility, collegiality, and adherence to the highest ethics make you a more effective lawyer. They help you win. In litigation, you cannot be a first-rate lawyer without them. Don't get me wrong. I am not saying that armed with courtesy and nothing else, you will be rewarded by judges and juries with one glorious victory after another.

Ours is a demanding craft. You have to master the skills of the craft. You have to be firm and courageous. And you must do all of the work needed, remembering that the poetry of a trial comes only from the drudgery of preparation. But if you do develop the skills, and put in the drudgery, the results you get will be better if you practice with courtesy and civility. Or, in other words, with "class."

Years ago I handled a plaintiff's malpractice case in which the client was a young child who had been damaged at birth. The doctor and hospital, we alleged, had bungled the delivery in a way that caused oxygen deprivation resulting in crippling injuries.

The doctor and the hospital were represented by excellent lawyers. In due course, I showed up in the city where the baby had been born to take the doctor's deposition. Before we could start, the doctor's lawyer took me aside.

"I want to tell you the good news about your case," he said.

"What's that?"

"The doctor altered the records," he said.

"Is that right?"

"Yes," said my opponent. "He panicked when the complaint was served and took out the record of this birth and made a false entry. I'll show you exactly what he did." And he showed me, on the medical chart, where the doctor had forged an entry to give his case an artificial boost.

"I thought you should see this now," said the lawyer, "so there could be no misunderstanding during the deposition."

What did the doctor's lawyer accomplish in this brief conversation? He discharged an ethical obligation. He disarmed me—I was denied the fun of turning up the false entry by asking questions. And he built a bond of trust between us. The case was settled soon afterward.

That bond of trust is vital to success. You build it from the beginning of every case.

How do you do it? Of course, through competence—you must do your work well. But beyond that, you keep your discovery demands reasonable, set depositions and other dates by agreement, act courteously to witnesses and get the job done quickly, never obstruct the process, and always keep your word.

The results are that you get your case well prepared with a minimum of expense and delay; opposing counsel nearly always become your friends; and both sides develop a willingness to deal with each other. That willingness to deal is of great practical importance. About 90 percent of all civil cases are resolved without trial. The same is true of criminal cases. The ability to negotiate a favorable settlement—the earlier, the better—is as important as the ability to try a case.

Now, who is going to do better at settling? The lawyer who has caused the other side to think of him as Atilla the Hun and who has drawn the other side into a "not-one-dime-for-that-s.o.b." mentality; or, the lawyer whose handling of the case has caused the other side to feel that "Here is a strong but civilized person—here, we can reason together"?

Perhaps the finest utterance to come out of the United States Senate since World War II—not an era of great eloquence, I will admit—was provided by the late Everett Dirksen of Illinois. "The oil can," he said, "is mightier than the sword." It is true in law as in politics.

How do you build that bond of trust if opposing counsel refuses to cooperate and subjects you to a steady diet of false accusations, nasty remarks, broken promises, and obstructionism? It's very simple: You respond with unremitting courtesy and good cheer. If insulted, you say something like: "Oh, you don't really mean that," and you get on with the work at hand.

Of course, you must be firm about getting what you're entitled to. But, while being firm, you should remember that inside every nasty, vicious lawyer is a principled, courteous lawyer trying to get out. Refuse to be convinced otherwise; it nearly always works.

Then there is the matter of just deserts—"poetic justice," as it's called.

Fanaticism and obstructionism are very unpopular with judges.

A lawyer who obstructs, who breaks or bends the rules, who treats his opponent uncivilly, is sending a message to the judge's subconscious: "Rule against me if you can." Judges do their best to resist such messages, but they are human. Most of them are, anyway.

And a lawyer's fanaticism tends to ruin the witnesses on his side. A client who sees his lawyer cheating on the rules begins to lose believability. A lawyer who beats rote answers into his client's head—who insists that the client never admit a thing against his position—erodes that client's believability.

Our trial system is a quest for the truth. Triers of fact look for truthfulness above all else. They sense when a person is leveling with them, and when not. Discourtesy and extremism repel them. It's not just that people dislike bad manners; it's that they know fanaticism is inconsistent with truth.

A while back a party to a civil suit in my court was testifying on cross-examination. He was relaxed and candid. He spoke well on the strong points of his case and admitted adverse facts when they should be admitted. The jury, I could sense, was with him. The noon recess arrived and I excused everyone for ninety minutes. After lunch the cross-examination resumed. The witness now was argumentative and evasive. If the truth was against him he would sidestep and counterpunch without answering the question. The jury's trust in him almost visibly drained away.

Does anyone have the slightest doubt about what happened over the lunch break?

Juries and judges are not just put off, but oppressed, by single-minded fanaticism. To have to sort through exaggerated claims and defenses hour after hour—to have to take everything that is said with a whole cellarful of salt—is hard work. Triers of fact are fair, but they cannot be pleased with those who subject them to such a grind.

The winning edge in trial advocacy is the ability to cause the jury to *want* to come out in your favor. Many advocates have the basic skills and industry, but lack that winning edge. Those who have it know that juries and judges are human; that they sense who behaves decently and who does not; and that reasonableness and fairness are at the heart of the matter.

I remember a time years ago when my client, the husband in a bitter divorce action, was on the stand. This was in the "good old days" when you had to prove grounds for divorce, putting a lot more spice into the proceedings than we have now. On direct examination, we came to a question that called on my client to tell about something really bad his wife had done. We had already shown grounds, but this would be the coup de grace.

I asked the question. There was a pause. My client turned to the judge and said: "I'd rather not talk about that, Your Honor. Do I have to?"

This was entirely spontaneous. If rehearsed, it could have been a disaster; in the event, it was a triumph. You could almost feel the judge's heart warming. He said, "That's up to Lawyer." Belatedly, I had enough sense to say, "I withdraw the question."

In another case, my client was a professional man—a very good one—who had done something wrong. His act reflected a horrendous lapse of judgment. Did it reflect something still worse? That issue had brought us into the courtroom.

In pre-trial interviews, the client had never been able to give a good explanation of why he had committed this folly. At trial, which was to the court, he was questioned by counsel. Then the judge asked him a simple question: "Why did you do it?" And the answer burst forth as from a collapsing dam: "I don't know! I don't know why I did it. I've thought about it a thousand times since, and I just don't know!"

As a text—as a matter of logic and relevance—this answer got us nowhere. But the courtroom is an arena not just of logic but of emotions. The answer carried the day, because it sounded like the cry of a man who had wounded himself where it hurt most—in his sense of honor—and was still feeling the pain of it.

These two examples do not show any special skill of counsel. They merely show what can happen when witnesses are free to be people—to be themselves.

And what does that have to do with ethics, courtesy, and civility? Just this: If a lawyer practices with honesty, decency, and good humor, her witnesses will do better, her trials will be better, her victories will be more frequent, and her settlements will come more easily.

So the Motherhood Reason for ethics is strong, as reflected these days in guidelines and codes of conduct adopted throughout the United States.

The Mirror Reason is also strong. We would all rather see Atticus Finch or Portia than the depraved Dorian Gray in the looking glass.

I have suggested another reason—the Mundane Reason. It's very simple: Courtesy and civility and ethics, when combined with skill and industry, bring the greatest measure of success.

So there is everything to gain, and nothing to lose. Or, to put it another way: Lawyers of the world, unite! You have nothing to lose but your dyspepsia.

NOTE

1 *Taming of the Shrew*, I, ii.

Finding the Center

D EAN LOH, JUDGE JONES, MEMBERS OF THE FACULTY, distinguished guests, ladies and gentlemen:[1]

I am deeply honored by your award, and I accept it with profound gratitude. Also with some degree of surprise, for two reasons.

The first is that I had always thought the greatest anticlimax in the world was that old song lyric, "For God, for country, and for Yale." But looking at the list of distinguished graduates who have received this award in the past, and seeing my name appended at the end, I realize that a new record has been set in the anti-climax league.

The second reason for surprise is that I do not hold a law degree from the University of Washington. When John Michalik wrote to tell me of the award,[2] I called him right away and pointed out that although I started law school at Washington in 1949 and was around, more or less, for three years, I finished up at New York University, which is where my law degree is from. Not being a graduate of the

53

law school, I asked, how could I be alumnus of the year? "Not a problem," said John without a moment's hesitation. "Don't give it a thought." At first I thought this was just another sign of the suppleness of Michalik's legal mind, a quality with which I was well familiar from the time of our joint service with the Washington State Bar Association. Then I consulted *Webster's New World Dictionary* and found that "alumnus" is defined as "a person who has attended or is a graduate of a particular school, college, or university." And on this narrow technical basis, I am able to accept your award not just with humility and gratitude, but even with a moderately clear conscience.

I am invited to give you a message tonight, and my guess is that you would prefer a message of good cheer. I am glad to do that—not just because good cheer is a tonic, but because I believe we have reason to be cheerful, even in what most of us see as difficult times.

I want to talk to you about the center.

Thoughtful Americans—thoughtful people everywhere in Western society—are feeling and bemoaning the loss of the center that is vital to civilized life. By the center I mean a shared set of beliefs and values providing coherence, morale, and inspiration.

Ever since the calamity of World War I we have been missing it. Probably the most unforgettable lines of poetry written in this century are these by William Butler Yeats:

> Things fall apart; the center cannot hold;
> Mere anarchy is loosed upon the world,
> The blood-dimmed tide is loosed, and everywhere
> The ceremony of innocence is drowned;
> The best lack all conviction, while the worst
> Are full of passionate intensity.[3]

Yeats published that in 1921, and the words have haunted us since, because they are beautiful, terrible, and largely true.

The same thought has been repeated many times in more prosaic terms. Kenneth Clark wound up his wonderful television series called *Civilisation* with this thought: "The trouble is that there is still no centre. The moral and intellectual failure of Marxism has left us with no alternative to heroic materialism, and that isn't enough."[4] So said Lord Clark after showing us thirteen hours of painting, sculpture, and architecture from which he omitted, conspicuously, twentieth-century art.

And what are the symptoms of this loss of a center? We know them all too well: low public morale, or, in other words, a failure of confidence; restless dissatisfaction even amid prosperity and freedom; mindless violence in the streets and in many homes; a vulgar and nasty tone in political life; the exaltation of personal ambition over the public good; cynicism about public institutions; and a tendency of society to splinter along lines of economic interest, race, ethnicity, and religious belief.

It is not a pretty picture. And nearly all who have thought about it agree that we can turn this oil-bespattered canvas into a landscape only if we find a new center.

In some earlier times the center has been provided by a dominant and official religion. So it was in the European Middle Ages. We can see latter-day versions of this in a few parts of the world where fundamentalist religion and the government are combined—in Iran, for example. Very few in the Western democracies would find such a regime appealing.

Another, more recent, center has been the shared commitment to economic development and material progress. That is still regarded as good, but as we contemplate the wreckage left by rampant industrialization in, for example, Eastern Europe, we see that it is not enough in itself.

And then, of course, there is always war—a kind of narcotic center for society; not good for us, and providing only a short-term high.

Where, then, should we turn?

I suggest that we have a center now, and we should look to it first. That center is the rule of law.

By the rule of law I do not just mean law and order, although that is important, but much more. I mean equality before the law, access to the law, and freedom under the law. I mean the jury system, the Bill of Rights, constitutional liberty, and justice provided through a fair, honest, and open court system.

This is the core value in which nearly all Americans believe: the value of justice; the value of liberty in a just society.

We see that belief in action every day. We see it in civil cases where the parties bring their disputes to court—everything from car accidents to divorce to antitrust litigation—have their contest, get their hearing, and abide by the results.

We see it in criminal trials where the accused has the benefit or the right to counsel and the presumption of innocence. We see it in the work of lawyers, thousands of whom, young and old, are idealists.

And we see it—above all, to my mind—in the work of juries. The jury is our most successful democratic institution. It works better than the ballot box, better than the initiative and referendum. Jurors take their jobs seriously. By and large they listen carefully, debate honestly, and decide intelligently and fairly. They do this even when the subject matter is difficult, and even where the unpopular or the despised are on trial. People want justice, yes. But they also want to *do* justice. They want justice for everyone—not just for themselves— and they are willing to work and sacrifice to provide it.

This—the rule of law—is our center. Or, more exactly, it is the core of our future center. It is alive, strong, and flourishing. And we lawyers in the United States have the great privilege of working, every day, exactly at the heart of our society.

Is this value shared elsewhere in the world? It is and it is growing. "Law is the ligament which holds civilized beings and civilized nations together," said our colleague Daniel Webster.

What Webster said a hundred and sixty years ago is even truer today. International law is growing in strength. The international human rights movement has been one of the quietest but most important changes in our time.

Is the rule of law itself enough? No, it will have to be accompanied by a broader ethic, a shared source of confidence and inspiration. Just what that will be I will have to leave to next year's speaker. But the rule of law should be enough to get us through the trough we are in. Whatever comes next, law will be the center of our center.

Well, as my partner Murray Guterson used to tell criminal defendants after advising them how to get their lives straightened out, there is no extra charge for the philosophy.[5]

It has been a pleasure to meet with you tonight, and I will cherish your award. Thank you.

NOTES

1 Dean Wallace Loh, University of Washington School of Law; Judge Richard Jones, King County Superior Court (in 2007, recommended by a bi-partisan panel to fill a vacancy on the U.S. District Court for the Western District of Washington).

2 John Michalik served as assistant dean for development at the University of Washington School of Law from 1991 to 1995.

3 Yeats, *The Second Coming and Other Poems* (Los Angeles: Plantin Press, 1970).

4 Kenneth Clark, *Civilisation: A Personal View* (New York: Harper and Row, 1969).

5 Murray Guterson was Bill Dwyer's long-time law partner.

Remarks on Semi-Retiring

December 1998

E LEVEN YEARS AGO AT THIS BANQUET THE FEDERAL Bar Association gave me a warm welcome to the bench. Tonight's greeting seems even warmer. I can only assume that the bar is even happier about my departure than it was about my arrival.

I want to reward your hospitality and generosity by not making a speech. But I would like to make a token payment on a huge debt of gratitude.

I believe there is only so much good luck in the world. Nobody understands how or why it is parceled out, but we know that some people fall into inordinate quantities of it while others seem to miss out altogether. In every way, I have been one of those lucky ones.

I'd like to thank just a few of the many who deserve to be thanked:

I am grateful to my wife, Vasiliki, and to our three children and three children-in-law and five very young grandchildren, for a remarkably happy home life.

To my long-suffering teachers, especially those at the University of Washington School of Law, who taught me a great deal more than must have been apparent at the time.

To the negotiators who signed the Korean War cease-fire agreement in 1953 in the same month that I got drafted.

To my superior officers in the army in occupied Germany, who let me try a great variety of court-martial cases.

To my law partners, Gordon Culp and Murray Guterson and George Grader, and all the other colleagues and fellow workers at the law firm that was my second family for thirty years.

To my colleagues and the staff members at the King County Bar Association and the Washington State Bar Association, from whom I learned a great deal while serving as a board member, and whose company was always a pleasure. To my friends at the U.S. Courthouse: Trish Graham, my secretary and chambers manager; Eileen Scollard, my in-court deputy clerk; and Mary Duett, my docket clerk—without all of whom nothing would be accomplished; the sixteen law clerks and seventy-five externs who have inspired me with their intellect and idealism; to our unsurpassed district executive, Bruce Rifkin, and all his deputies; to Marshal Rosa Melendez and her colleagues in the marshal's office; to chief probation officer Bob Lee and his fellow officers; and to all the district judges, magistrate judges, and bankruptcy judges of the district. In the history of our district there have been twenty-four federal district judges; I have known seventeen of them personally, starting with John Bowen, who was appointed by President Roosevelt, and continuing through Bob Lasnik, who took office just a few days ago. We could have no finer addition to the bench than Bob Lasnik.[1]

To the many citizens who have served faithfully as jurors in my court.

To the Ninth Circuit for correcting my errors (although they have detected only a small percentage of them).

To the Supreme Court for correcting the Ninth Circuit's errors.

To future Supreme Courts for correcting the current Supreme Court's errors (we all need review).

And especially, tonight, to the members of the bar. Our system of justice is the greatest in the world. It has three pillars: the jury; the independent judiciary; and a strong, ethical, and independent bar. Lawyers, I believe, are the unsung heroes of our society. It is fashionable to criticize lawyers, but most of the criticism is mistaken. Lawyers work faithfully to preserve constitutional liberties, to protect children and others who cannot protect themselves, to uphold the rights of the unpopular and the despised, to assure the law-abiding conduct of business in every sphere of activity, and to serve pro bono the needs of those who cannot afford to pay. You and I know that the chief reward of practicing law is not making money (although that does no harm) but the knowledge that you are helping clients and serving the cause of justice. We are all privileged to work in a great tradition. In this district that tradition has always been fully honored by the bar. And for all of my time on the bench, the bar has made the job of judging not just a privilege but a pleasure.

Thank you for that.

This is not quite a farewell because although I have been on senior status for the past week, I plan to keep a full caseload until my successor arrives, and then move to part-time work. So this is not goodbye but just so long. Or, as the saying goes, I'll see you in court.

1 The judges serving prior to Judge Lasnik in the Western District of
Washington are, with dates of active service (excluding any periods serving
on senior status), listed in order of appointment:

Cornelius Holgate Hanford,
    1905–1912
George Donworth, 1909–1912
Edward E. Cushman, 1912–1939
Clinton W. Howard, 1912–1913
Jeremiah Neterer, 1913–1933
John Clyde Bowen, 1934–1961
Lloyd Llewellyn Black, 1939–1950
Charles Henry Leavy, 1942–1952
William James Lindberg, 1951–1971
George Hugo Boldt, 1953–1971
William Trulock Beeks, 1961–1973
William Nelson Goodwin,
    1966–1975

Walter Thomas McGovern,
    1971–1987
Morell Edward Sharp, 1971–1980
Donald S. Voorhees, 1974–1986
Jack Edward Tanner, 1978–1991
Barbara Jacobs Rothstein, 1980–2003
John C. Coughenour, 1981–2006
Carolyn R. Dimmick, 1985–1997
Robert Jensen Bryan, 1986–2000
William Lee Dwyer, 1987–1998
Thomas Samuel Zilly, 1988–2004
Franklin D. Burgess, 1994–2005
Robert S. Lasnik, 1998–

NOTE: In 2003, Judge Barbara Rothstein was named Director of the
Federal Judicial Center in Washington, D.C., a research and education
agency for the federal judicial system. Her appointment to this position
is for a period or four to seven years, after which she can resume her seat
as an active judge for the Western District of Washington. For more general
detail on the Western District Court, see *The U.S. District Court for the
Western District of Washington* (2004).

Lincoln Then and Now

LINCOLN DAY BANQUET

TACOMA-PIERCE COUNTY BAR ASSOCIATION

February 11, 1999

I T IS A GREAT PLEASURE TO BE IN TACOMA AGAIN. I have happy memories here. When I was a trial lawyer, I tried a good many cases before judges and juries in Tacoma. In federal court, I came before Judges George Boldt and Bill Goodwin. In superior court, I worked with Judges Horace Geer, Billy Richmond, Stanley Worswick, and others.[1] If that sounds like an all-male cast, it was; this was before the full-scale entry of women into the legal profession, which has taken place, happily, over the past generation.

I always enjoyed those trials, and I enjoyed living here. One of the trials took so long that my wife, Vasiliki, and I moved here and spent several weeks living at the old Winthrop Hotel, a grand place. I suppose it is a mark of Tacoma's progress that the Winthrop is now devoted to subsidized housing and more modern hotels have taken its place.

And so it has been with the old federal courthouse, which I thought was a fine place to try cases but which has now been replaced by one of the most beautiful courthouses ever built in the United States, the Union Station Courthouse. Many people deserve credit for that achievement, but in the judiciary the main credit goes to Judge Bob Bryan, whose prodigious work on the project has earned our ever-lasting thanks.

It was in 1988 that I first had the honor of speaking at the Tacoma-Pierce County Lincoln Day Banquet. In the eleven years since that night many things have changed. I have aged by twenty-two years; my wife has gotten younger; all three of our children have married and produced children of their own.

Your own lives, I am sure, have been filled with changes as well—with happy ones, I hope.

But some things have not changed at all. The legal profession is still a bastion of justice and democracy in the United States; the jury system still works better than any other democratic institution; and this banquet remains one of the foremost annual events in the Pacific Northwest.

When your committee invited me to come back, I accepted gladly with one condition: that I would give a revised version of the speech I gave the first time, entitled "Lincoln Then and Now." The committee accepted the condition, probably in the well-founded belief that no one would remember a word I had said eleven years ago. But if you happened to be here in 1988 and miraculously remember the talk, please feel free to adjourn to the nearby bar. I do assure you, though, that tonight's version will be shorter and will have more of Lincoln and less of the guest speaker.

This is the ninety-first Lincoln Day Banquet. Why have we done this? Why has the Pierce County bar chosen to honor this man, Abraham Lincoln, so often and for so long?

One reason is that Lincoln was one of us. He was a lawyer. He was a trial lawyer. He was the best lawyer ever to serve as president of the United States. And, of course, it follows as the night follows the day, he was also the best president.

But the main reason for this celebration is that Lincoln personifies what we want our country to mean and to stand for. He was born a backwoodsman. He had a grand total of about one year of school. Yet in all the history of the world no braver, nobler, or more humane man has ever led a nation through its supreme crisis.

We still miss Lincoln—especially when election years approach. Suppose he were to come back today, alive, and enter the field of candidates now shaping up for the 2000 presidential election. What would he do? What would he say? And how would we react to him?

Let us imagine his arrival. He is now fifty-one years old as he was when he first ran for president in 1860. What would strike us about this man? We would notice that he is six feet four inches tall. He is on the skinny side. He has a high-pitched, metallic voice. In appearance he could fairly be called homely—tall, lank, with drooping eyelids. His hands would impress us as looking awkward. Some of his movements would look awkward. We would soon find out, the press being as diligent as it is these days, that his feet hurt a good deal of the time.

He was a man who spoke plainly, and he spoke with an accent. As one biographer describes it:

A southern Indiana dialect affected much of Lincoln's speech all his life. Like his neighbors, young Lincoln said 'howdy' to visitors. He "sot" down and "stayed a spell." He came "outen" a cabin and "yearned" his wages and made a heap. He "cum" from "whar" he had been. He was "hornswoggled" into doing something against his better judgment. He "keered" for his friends and "heered" the latest news. He pointed to "yonder" stream and addressed the head of a committee as "Mr. Cheermun."[2]

By the standards of his own time, Lincoln was widely thought to lack what was called dignity. He did have some habits that were irritating to Mrs. Lincoln. He liked to read newspapers aloud to himself.

He was a careless dresser. His feet were often on the desk or chair or whatever else was elevated.

He was absent-minded. He once took one of the young Lincoln children out for a walk, towing the boy in a wagon behind him. The child fell off, but Lincoln did not notice. Deep in thought, he walked on for block after block, towing the empty wagon through the streets of Springfield, Illinois.

He was a fine lawyer, but a slipshod record keeper. One visitor to the office of Lincoln and Herndon claimed that seeds were sprouting in the cracks between the floorboards.

Unlike many men of his time, Lincoln did not hunt, did not fish, and did not drink. But he had no objection to others doing any of these things. He relished the company of men. He loved to tell stories, and he loved to hear them.

He had three moods. There was the mood of exuberance and laughter. There was the working mood, in which he was totally absorbed with what he was doing, especially during court trials. And there was what he called "the hypo." The hypo was his mood of black depression, and he suffered from bouts of it all his life.

In those harder times, Lincoln suffered the deaths of his mother at a young age; of his only brother in infancy; of his only sister when she was twenty-one; of his beloved friend Ann Rutledge when she was twenty-two; and, eventually, of two of his own young sons.

He had a literary gift. He wrote some poetry himself, but his favorite verse was by a Scotsman by the name of William Knox. The poem is called "Mortality," and it amounts to a profoundly sad comment on the human condition. Lincoln often quoted it, and sometimes he would mutter the words to himself as he stared out a window. In this poem, the word "bier" refers not to the popular beverage but to a platform on which a coffin is placed. The poem closes with this stanza:

> 'Tis the wink of an eye, 'tis the draught of a breath
> From the blossoms of health, to the paleness of death

From the gilded saloon, to the bier and the shroud
Oh, why should the spirit of mortal be proud![3]

Although he had strong religious feelings, Lincoln never joined a church.

In the mid-nineteenth century there was no undue exposure of marital details, and to this day the quality of Lincoln's marriage is largely a mystery. The *Macmillan Dictionary of Biographv* says that he and Mary Todd were "temperamentally unsuited" and had an "unhappy marriage." Meantime, the *Dictionary of American Biography* says that "their marriage seems to have been a happy one, their love for each other deep and sincere."

What we do know with certainty is that Lincoln as a young man thought he would never marry because he was too awkward and shy with women. He anticipated Groucho Marx by a century when he said, "I can never be satisfied with anyone who would be blockhead enough to have me."

He courted Mary Todd without much hope before their marriage. He pointed out that God only needed one "d" to spell his name whereas the Todds needed two. For a long time, the Todd family rejected Lincoln because he was beneath their station.

He came from a family of poor homesteaders. His mother and father were illiterate. As a boy and young man Lincoln cut timber, split fence rails, plowed, threshed wheat, and hired out to other homesteaders and gave the wages to his father. He worked as a riverboat man. He became a renowned ax-swinger. He was a fine wrestler.

He had a reputation for a time of hanging around with ruffians. But he was a ruffian with a difference, because in him there was the soul of a poet. He learned how to read. He read deeply the few books he could find—especially Shakespeare, the Bible, and the political document we call the Declaration of Independence.

He became a store clerk and a part-time surveyor. He opened a store with a partner. The business did not prosper. They ran up what

Lincoln called, for years afterward, "the national debt." Eventually he paid it all off. He volunteered and served in the Blackhawk Indian War.[4] He never claimed more for this military service than that he had survived, as he put it, "a good many blood struggles with mosquitoes."

Then came the great turning point. Lincoln became a lawyer. He was self-taught. He became a lawyer by reading the books to himself and then taking a brief oral bar exam, after which he took the three lawyers who had examined him out to dinner.

It was the law that opened the world to Abraham Lincoln, and our profession can take special pride in him. He became one of the best practicing lawyers in Illinois. He practiced law for twenty-three years. He rode the circuit of the smaller towns on horseback, trying cases of all kinds: murder cases, collection suits, railroad battles, torts, contracts, larceny defenses. Although it was said of our profession that lawyers who defended horse thieves always, for some reason, were very well mounted, Lincoln never rode a noteworthy horse.

He was a friendly, capable adversary who spoke in plain words. He once gave advice to would-be lawyers: "There is a vague popular belief that lawyers are necessarily dishonest ... [Do not] yield to this popular belief. Resolve to be honest at all events; and if in your own judgment, you cannot be an honest lawyer, resolve to be honest without being a lawyer."[5]

Other lawyers practicing in Illinois said Lincoln was unsurpassed in working with a jury. He did have certain biases, as many trial lawyers do. He believed that fat men were ideal jurors because they were jolly by nature and easily swayed. He rejected people with high foreheads because he thought they had already made up their minds. And he considered blond, blue-eyed males to be inherently nervous and likely to side with the prosecution.

The most famous story about Lincoln as a trial lawyer is the one in which he was defending a neighbor charged with murder. A prosecution witness claimed to have seen the deed done by moonlight.

Lincoln then drew the witness out about the brilliance of the moon-light, and then pulled out an almanac showing that the night in question was dark with barely a sliver of late-rising moon. The witness was discredited. The defendant was acquitted. And, ladies and gentlemen, the story is true.

But the story I like best about Lincoln as a trial lawyer concerns a much more obscure case. He represented a man who had sold a team of oxen and a plow to two young men. The two young buyers had given a promissory note in payment. They were both under age, as it happened. They soon defaulted on the note and Lincoln's client sued to collect. The defense, of course, was infancy—lack of capacity to make a promissory note.

The evidence came in, and Lincoln gave his closing argument. He pointed out that the young men had received full value—the plow and the team of oxen were worth the amount of the note. The defense of infancy, he said, should not be used to facilitate cheating. Then he took a tack which exemplifies our profession at its best. He turned the appeal for his client into an appeal for the two young buyers. He told the jurors they should not do a disservice to these two young men. "Gentlemen of the jury," he said, "are you willing to allow these boys to begin life with this shame and disgrace attached to their character?" He meant the shame of evading a just debt. And he quoted Shakespeare:

> Good name in man and woman, dear my lord,
> Is the immediate jewel of their souls:
> Who steals my purse steals trash; 'tis something, nothing;
> 'Twas mine, 'tis his, and has been slave to thousands;
> But he that filches from me my good name
> Robs me of that which not enriches him,
> And makes me poor indeed.[6]

The jury saved the character of the two young men, and Lincoln's client won his case.

In trial Lincoln took no notes, yet he could marshal the evidence in detail in closing argument. In a day of few appellate precedents, he became a leading appeals court lawyer. He handled 243 cases before the Illinois Supreme Court. He followed the golden rule of brevity in writing. When asked once to comment on another lawyer's windy brief, Lincoln said, "He got to writing and was too lazy to stop."

When he left Springfield, one hundred and thirty-eight years ago today, to go to Washington to be president, he told his law partner Billy Herndon, "Give our clients to understand that the election of a President makes no change in the firm of Lincoln and Herndon."

By the age of fifty, he had been active a long time in politics, with mixed results. In his early twenties he ran for the state legislature. He said that if the people elected him he would regard it as a favor. If not, "I have been too familiar with disappointments to be very much chagrined." He lost.

In later years he did serve, with distinction, in the state legislature. In the 1840s he served one term in the United States House of Representatives, where he voted against the war with Mexico, saying it was unjust and had been started by our government on a pretext. When his term was nearly up, he said "I neither seek, expect, nor deserve a second term."

In 1858 he ran for the Senate. He had the famous series of debates with Stephen Douglas over the slavery issue. Lincoln said he had often heard arguments from people who maintained that slavery was a good thing, but he had never met a man who wanted to try out this good thing by becoming a slave himself. Lincoln was widely known by now but he had no delusions of grandeur. When Douglas accused him of being two-faced, Lincoln answered: "I leave it to my audience. If I had another face, do you think I'd wear this one?

Again he lost. And he said, "I feel like the boy who stubbed his toe—I am too big to cry and too badly hurt to laugh."

By 1860, he was renowned as a speaker. In his shrill voice, he could argue forcefully, cogently, and with great convincing power.

But by the standards of 1999 he certainly would not be telegenic. Picture, then, this man as a candidate for president. What would he do? Well, in the first place he would not lie. And he would not make a speech saying he wasn't going to lie; he just wouldn't do it. He would not smile excessively. These days, every campaign seems to be sponsored by the American Dental Association.

He was used to the tradition of real political speeches, long speeches. They amounted to a kind of open-air theater. People would come from miles around to listen to political orators. (This, of course, was before television reduced our attention span to thirty seconds.) Lincoln would prefer these long set-pieces to an exchange of slogans. But in a contest of one-liners, he would win; he would certainly win if everybody had to make up his own one-liners.

He would respond with wit and kindness to personal attacks against him.

And he would speak to the issues that he saw as important whether or not they were on the table for public debate at the time.

Beyond these generalities, do you really think I am fool enough to believe I could tell you exactly what Lincoln would say on the complex and profound issues of our day? Of course I am. How do you think federal judges are picked? But as fate would have it, I cannot tell you, because the canons of judicial ethics prohibit me from making a political speech.

What I can say, and it is true, is that Lincoln would appeal to the best in us. He would argue with force and logic, and he would speak to our reason, our decency, and our common humanity.

How would we react to him? Would we be able to see any of his greatness? Would he get past the polls, the Iowa caucuses, New Hampshire, and Super Tuesday?

If you feel as skeptical about the answers to those questions as I do, perhaps we can take some comfort in the knowledge that his quality was not widely recognized in 1860 either. While Lincoln was running for president, he was called such names as "ass," "huckster," "lunatic," "mobocrat," "bloodthirsty tyrant," and "chimpanzee." He never held a grudge. He said it didn't pay to hold grudges.

He was elected with 39 percent of the vote because the Democratic vote was split three ways. And six weeks after the election, South Carolina seceded, the other southern states followed, and the Civil War was on.

The war proved more terrible than anyone imagined. It seemed endless. Lincoln was faced with a crushing series of military defeats; the heartbreaking loss of thousands of young men; generals who were incompetent; an unpopular draft; riots in northern cities; demands for compromise with the South.

But he saw what was at stake—the fate of democratic government. He said, "We can nobly save, or meanly lose, the last best hope of earth."[7]

Even as the war aged him, as we see in his face in the photographs, he never lost his sense of humor. He was always beset by a horde of office-seekers. In 1863 he came down with a mild form of smallpox, and he said, "Now I have something I can give everybody."

By 1864 Lincoln was unpopular and stridently criticized from all sides. Hundreds of thousands had been killed. No end was in sight. There was a movement in his own party to nominate John C. Frémont to replace him. Lincoln said Frémont reminded him of a fellow back home who was "the damndest scoundrel that ever lived, but in the infinite mercy of providence, he was also the damndest fool."

It seemed certain in 1864 that he would lose the election, but in the nick of time came victories—victories under General Ulysses S. Grant and General William Tecumseh Sherman. And with the victories on the battlefield, the political tide turned and Abraham Lincoln was re-elected.

Lincoln wrote every word of his own speeches. In his second inaugural address, late in the war, when victory at last was in sight, he spoke in his merciful and good-hearted way about rebuilding the country: "With malice toward none; with charity for all, with firmness in the right as God gives us to see the right, let us strive on to finish the work we are in, to bind up the nation's wounds; . . . to do all which may achieve and cherish a just and lasting peace."[8] He did not live to do that work.

Abraham Lincoln was imperfect, as all men are imperfect. But the shorthand description that we learned in school—he saved the Union and freed the slaves—is largely true.

He guided us through our greatest struggle and kept our ideals alive through four years of fratricide. On the slavery issue he progressed from opposing the extension of slavery, to the Emancipation Proclamation which abolished it in the South, to backing the Thirteenth Amendment which ended it throughout the country forever. He led us out of the wilderness of our own darkest impulses, and left us the sunlight of his words.

Lincoln became one of the last casualties of our most terrible war. Many who were killed then, as in any war, had no idea why they died. But Lincoln expected to lose his life, and he knew why he was willing to give it.

We honor him first among the many who fell. And let us always remember what he asked us to do, in a message as beautiful and urgent today as when he first delivered it on the battlefield of Gettysburg:

. . . that from these honored dead we take increased devotion to that cause for which they gave the last full measure of devotion; that we here highly resolve that these dead shall not have died in vain; that this nation, under God, shall have a new birth of freedom; and that government of the people, by the people, for the people, shall not perish from the earth.[9]

1 Horace G. Greer served as a Pierce County Superior Court Judge from 1966 to 1975. On the same court, W. A Richmond served from 1948 to 1961 and Stanley W. Worswick, from 1969 to 1981.

2 Stephen Oates, *With Malice toward None: The Life of Abraham Lincoln* (Harper & Row, 1977), p. 12.

3 From *The Lonely Hearth, the Songs of Israel, Harp of Sion, and Other Poems*, 1847.

4 Lincoln volunteered in 1832. See *Encyclopedia Britannica*, "Abraham Lincoln" (childhood and youth).

5 Fred R. Shapiro, *Oxford Dictionary of Legal Quotations*, 1993, p. 128.

6 *Othello*, 3.iii.155. For more on this trial, see Richard H. Underwood, "Moonlight: Abraham Lincoln and the Almanac Trial," 29 N. Ky. L. Rev. 237 (2002).

7 Lincoln's Second Annual Message to Congress, in *Abraham Lincoln: Speeches and Writings, 1859–1865* (Library of America, 1989), p. 415.

8 Second Inaugural Address, March 4, 1865, *Oxford Dictionary of Quotations*.

9 Lincoln's Address at Gettysburg, November 19, 1863.

Centennial Expectations

SCHOOL OF LAW COMMENCEMENT

UNIVERSITY OF WASHINGTON

June 13, 1999

D EAN HJORTH,[1] MEMBERS OF THE FACULTY, HONORED guests, new graduates, parents and friends. It is a great pleasure and honor to speak to you on this happy day.

This is a moment that calls for a look at the big picture. The first thing I notice about that picture is that fifty years have sped by since my classmates and I began law school at the University of Washington. It was the fall of 1949. The world's population was less than half what it is now; NATO was formed that year; the Communists took over China after a long civil war; the Russians, to our great alarm, tested an atomic bomb; George Orwell's book *1984* was published; there was still officially imposed segregation in the United States (*Brown v. Board of Education* would not come down for another five years);[2] and the Yankees beat Brooklyn in the World Series, four games to one. (Brooklyn was the home of the Dodgers, and in a more perfect society it still would be.)

Our class was diverse in terms of age. Some were World War II veterans—savvy, mature, and focused on what they wanted to do, which was to graduate from law school as quickly as possible. Others, myself included, were young and ignorant and had wandered into old Condon Hall more or less on the theory that everybody has to be somewhere. But in other ways we were not diverse. We were almost entirely a group of white males; there were only three women and one student of color. Anyone who doubts that progress can be made should compare the makeup of our class and the one graduating today.

Some other things have changed too. These days it is very hard to get into a first-rate law school, but the student, once admitted, is nurtured toward a happy ending. Half a century ago, the University of Washington, like other law schools, operated on a survival-of-the-fittest basis: it was easy to get in but hard to get out in one piece. About half of the first-year class was flunked out. Another large contingent was cut loose in the second year. By the end of the third year, a little band of haggard survivors remained. We had learned a great deal. We had learned from professors who used the Socratic method to instill some mental rigor in our soft heads. Like any group that struggles together through a common ordeal, we students bonded and became friends. To this day, some of my best friends are fellow survivors of that law school class. Only later did we realize how good our training had been. This was a fine law school back then; today it is a great one, and in your century it will be even greater.

We are here to celebrate, but beyond congratulating you who have just earned your law degrees, I want to tell you a little about what you are getting into—about what you can expect as lawyers in the twenty-first century.

You will learn, first of all, that to be a lawyer is to make mistakes. If you yearn for perfection, that's fine; you can spend a lifetime seeking it in the law. The chase can be thrilling and rewarding. But if you can't stand the pain of having made a mistake right in front of everybody, you might be better off making ceramic pottery, where you can break up your errors into small fragments and hide them in the trash can.

Since we are all imperfect, and language is imperfect, some of your mistakes will be made in the use of English. This is inevitable and not to be feared.

There was the lawyer in my court who indignantly answered his opponent's argument by saying, "Your honor, there's a red herring I would like to put to bed." There was the lawyer who wrote, in a maritime case involving a shipboard winch, that his client specialized in manufacturing "trawl wenches"—a type of female deckhand, apparently. There was the criminal defense lawyer who insisted that his client was being made an "escape goat." Realizing that didn't sound right, he corrected it by saying his client was being made a "scape-goat."

Sometimes you will be able to turn your verbal debacles to advantage. Years ago a good friend of mine, J. Marvin Jonsson, was trying a case to a jury in Seattle.[3] Mr. Jonsson was and is an excellent trial lawyer. Nevertheless, he found in this trial, suddenly and to his alarm and surprise, that he had to call himself as a witness to prove a point for his client. So he said, "Your Honor, we call as our next witness J. Marvin Jonsson." He came forward, took the oath, took the stand, and began to ask himself questions. He asked: "What is your name?" He gave his name. He asked: "Where do you live?" He gave his address. He asked himself several more simple questions, and everything went smoothly. Then he did something we all do at times: he asked a question that got tangled up in dependent clauses and twisted syntax and gradually petered out in the mire. There was a pause, and Mr. Jonsson said: "I don't understand the question; would you mind rephrasing it?"

Yes, all of us lawyers trip over our native tongue. And yet to be a lawyer is to work in a tradition where language has been used as clearly, as pointedly, as beautifully as it ever has been used outside the realm of poetry. Take, for example, the great Chief Justice John Marshall, who set our constitutional course early in the nineteenth century, and who wrote: "We must never forget that it is a *constitution* we are expounding . . . a constitution intended to endure for ages to come, and consequently, to be adapted to the various crises of human affairs."[4] Those words still resound with us.

Or take the example of Justice Louis Brandeis, dissenting in the 1927 case of Anita Whitney, who had been found guilty of belonging to an organization that advocated what was called "criminal syndicalism" and sentenced to prison. Justice Brandeis wrote:

> Those who won our independence believed that the final end of the state was to make men free to develop their faculties; and that in its government the deliberative forces should prevail over the arbitrary. They valued liberty both as an end and as a means. They believed liberty to be the secret of happiness and courage to be the secret of liberty. They believed that freedom to think as you will and to speak as you think are means indispensable to the discovery and spread of political truth.[5]

Brandeis lost in 1927, but since then he and his words have carried the day. He did not have the literary gift of his friend and colleague, Oliver Wendell Holmes Jr. Brandeis worked at English prose—and by mastering it, he expanded his influence and effectiveness. Every lawyer, in his or her own way, can do the same.

You will find that there is no higher calling than the one you are in, and that the more faithfully you observe the canons of ethics and the ideal of professional civility, the more worldly success you will enjoy. This doesn't mean that you will succeed just by being courteous—you have to be good at what you do. But it does mean—and this is one of the basic truths of law practice—that the best rewards come to those who are not just capable but ethical.

You already know that plenty of hard work will be needed, that you should give heart and soul to the task, and that nights and weekends will be chewed up in the service of clients and cases. Overwork is part of our stock in trade. But you will find that time off—real time off, with your head as well as the rest of you miles away from the job—not only will be refreshing but will make you a better lawyer. When I was in private practice I tore myself away (it wasn't easy) for two sabbaticals: one in Spain for a year with my wife and two small children, and then, a decade later, a year-long trip around the world with the same wife and three larger children. We all figured out the meaning of life (of course we have forgotten it since); we saw the world; we had many laughs together; and we were sure that neither the clients nor anyone else would miss us too painfully. I remember coming back after a year's absence and hearing colleagues I ran into on the street say, "How've you been? Haven't seen you for a couple of weeks." It all worked so well that my firm adopted sabbaticals for everybody—lawyers, secretaries, paralegals, messengers—and everybody seized the opportunity and came back to work renewed. During your careers, sabbaticals will sweep the world.

In your century, in the United States, we still will have the adversary system, and trial by jury, but these will be improved to make trials speedier, fairer, and more affordable. Reforms to accomplish that are in the works; the bar must help them succeed. And alongside the adversary battle will be a thriving nationwide culture of mediation—a method of dispute resolution that quickly is becoming not the "alternative" but the standard.

You will encounter, as a lawyer, many examples of mankind puffed up with self righteousness and pride. You will notice this among opposing clients; opposing counsel (until you get to know them better); your own clients (until you get them straightened out); and even, if you are not careful, in yourself. You will come to appreciate the wisdom of our colleague Michel de Montaigne, the sixteenth-century French lawyer who became the greatest of essayists and who wrote:

"There is no man so good that if he placed all his actions and thoughts under the scrutiny of the laws, he would not deserve hanging ten times in his life.[6]

You will find that the gods are always on the lookout for hubris. They will reward you with more victories if you don't attribute the ones you have to your own prowess.

You will see in daily life, and in public life, over and again, the role that fear and cowardice play in human affairs. But you will see also that courage can turn disaster into triumph. You will be inspired if you remember the courage of Sir Thomas More, the lawyer who became a saint. Sir Thomas was condemned to death, on perjured testimony, by a court convened by King Henry VIII. Before being taken away and beheaded, he was given a chance to say a few words. Thomas More looked at his judges. "I verily trust," he said, "and shall therefore right heartily pray, that though your lordships have now here on earth been judges to my condemnation, we may yet hereafter in heaven merrily all meet together, to our everlasting salvation."[7] We should all depart with such good cheer.

You will see in your work that hatred and cruelty are still with us. But you will know that you are standing at the bar with Clarence Darrow, the great defense lawyer who, in the 1920s, late in his life, recaptured the idealism of his younger days. In the Loeb-Leopold case, Darrow pleaded for the lives of two young men against a tide of public opinion and a press clamoring for the death penalty. He told the court at the end of one of the finest arguments ever given: "If I can succeed, my greatest reward and my greatest hope will be that I have done something . . . to help human understanding, to temper justice with mercy, to overcome hate with love."[8]

Darrow didn't always win, but he did this time; the two young men were sentenced to life-plus-ninety-nine-years.

You will be a colleague of many who have struggled bravely for racial justice through law. Thurgood Marshall, to take one example, argued case after case to end officially sanctioned segregation and went on to become the first African American justice of the Supreme Court. Justice Marshall always remembered his roots and ours. "We must never forget," he said, "that the only real source of power that we as judges can tap is the respect of the people."[9]

You will enter a profession that is finally becoming open—fully open—to women. The battle has not been easy. Clara Foltz was the first woman lawyer in California. Deserted by her husband and left with five children, she gained a legal education and practiced against great obstacles for fifty years. A trial in San Francisco, in 1889, shows what she had to go through. She was defending a young Italian immigrant charged with arson. The evidence came in and then, in closing argument, the prosecutor denounced Mrs. Foltz. "She is a woman!" he said. "She cannot be expected to reason; God almighty decreed her limitations, but you [members of the jury] can reason." Clara Foltz replied:

> If your Honor please and gentlemen of the jury: . . . Counsel opened his argument with the astounding revelation that I am a woman. . . . I am a woman and I am a lawyer—and what of it? . . . I came into the practice of my profession under the laws of this State, regularly and honestly, and . . . I have come to stay. I am neither to be bullied out nor worn out. I ask no special privileges and expect no favors, but I think it only fair that those who have had better opportunities than I, who have had fewer obstacles to surmount and fewer difficulties to contend with should meet me on even ground, upon the merits of law and fact without this everlasting and incessant reference to sex. . . .[10]

The all-male jury returned a not-guilty verdict for Mrs. Foltz's client without leaving the box.

You will learn to give your client a sympathetic ear, to take the burden from your client's shoulders, to work in a good cause without pay, to answer the phone at two a.m. when a friend calls, with embarrassment, to say he needs to be bailed out of jail. (If you go downtown and bail him out, you will gain not only his gratitude but a new circle of acquaintances at the police station and the bail bond office.)

You already know that the best lawyers—the ones who work in the great tradition—put the interests of justice always before their own interests. Not everybody knows this, but the author and columnist Anthony Lewis does. He recently said:

> I have seen lawyers perform nobly—that is not too strong
> a word—in all kinds of cases over the decades, from those
> who defended supposed security risks in the McCarthy years
> to those who fight for immigrants and poor men and women
> on death row today. They have done so in many cases without
> compensation: financial compensation, that is. For there is
> compensation of another kind.[11]

Indeed there is, and you will be able to get as much of that other kind of compensation as you choose. And yet, as long as the present fad continues, you will have to listen to cynical remarks and bad jokes about the legal profession. There is not much use in getting angry at these. They stem from ignorance and it is better to treat them with kindness and friendly persuasion.

There was a similar public sentiment a hundred and fifty years ago. One of the best trial lawyers in Illinois answered it by saying: "There is a vague popular belief that lawyers are necessarily dishonest. . . . Let no young man choosing the law for a calling for a moment yield to the popular belief—resolve to be honest at all events; and if in your own judgment you cannot be an honest lawyer, resolve to be honest without being a lawyer."[12] That trial lawyer went on to become our greatest president—Abraham Lincoln.

I hope the quotations I have used will not give you the impression that all the best lawyers are dead. The truth is that you will be joining many thousands of lawyers in the United States, and throughout the world, who are honest, generous, good-humored, and public-spirited. You will find them in every walk of legal life. They try and settle cases with skill and integrity; they analyze business problems, draft contracts, and write wills with insight and clarity; they do pro bono work; they adjust insurance claims, prosecute or defend criminal cases, teach law, draft bills, or serve on the bench, with a wholehearted dedication to justice. Many of them will become your friends; many of your opponents, you will find, will become your friends.

It may have occurred to you that much of this talk could have been given to the graduating class of 1901. You would be right, but that is one of the beauties of our profession. Our tradition has been strong for a long time, and I hope that today's remarks will make sense at the commencement tentatively scheduled for June 2099.

There is one big difference, though, between what you can expect and what was clearly in sight a century ago. The greatest political development of this millennium has been the growth of the rule of law—the replacement of arbitrary, unpredictable, personal power with a regime of justice implemented through a legal system. That has come about in every advanced nation, in every well-ordered society. The great step in the next millennium—in fact, very early in the next millennium—must be to establish the rule of law world wide and among nations. This is already happening, through the work of international human rights courts, the ever growing appeals to international law, the formation of earth-saving treaties, and a variety of collective actions, however ragged and ill-organized some of them may be, that are designed to end aggression and atrocity. Step by step, the rule of law is gaining ground throughout the world. We lawyers have a responsibility to make sure it succeeds. Whatever kind of legal work you do, as long as you do it well and faithfully, you will be contributing to that great historic advance. There could be no finer opportunity. And you have earned it through the work and dedication that brought you here today.

As your working life goes on, you will find yourself remembering your teachers more often and more vividly than you might expect.
I witnessed a fine example of that not long ago while serving as a visiting judge with the Ninth Circuit Court of Appeals in San Francisco.
A lawyer, nettled by something his opponent had said, rose and replied
with great dignity: "If my old evidence professor were alive today,
he'd be turning over in his grave."

NOTES

1 Roland L. Hjorth served as dean of the University of Washington
School of Law from 1995 to 2001.

2 *Brown v. Board of Education*, 347 U.S. 483 (1954).

3 J. Marvin Jonsson is a Seattle lawyer and a 1954 graduate of the
University of Washington School of Law.

4 Justice Marshall quote: *McCulloch v. Maryland*, 17 U.S. 316, 407,
415 (1819).

5 *Whitney v. California*, 274 U.S. 357, 375 (1927) (Brandeis, J.,
concurring).

6 Montaigne, *Essays*, book 3, chap. 9 (1595).

7 See Edward McGlynn Gafney, Jr., "The Principled Resignation of
Thomas More," 31 *Loy. L.A. Law Rev.* 63 (1997).

8 Clarence Darrow's sentencing speech in *State of Illinois v. Leopold
and Loeb* (Professional Education Group, 1988).

9 This quotation from a speech by Justice Marshall was referred to by
Glen Elsasser and Nicholas M. Horrock in "A Giant Is Gone: Justice Marshall
Dies, Leaving Legacy of Equal Rights," *Chicago Tribune*, Jan. 25, 1993, p. 1.
Elsasser and Horrock noted that when Justice Marshall made the speech
(ca. 1981), he was frustrated with the Burger court, especially its imposition
of intent as an element of proof in discrimination cases and its tendency to
restrict the rights of criminal defendants. It was noted that the speech was
an obvious response to a speech by Justice Burger, who had criticized the
American criminal justice system for providing "massive safeguards for
accused persons." Beyond the language quoted by Judge Dwyer, Justice

Marshall went on to observe that "we will command that respect only as long as we strive for neutrality. If we are perceived as campaigning for particular policies, as joining with other branches of government in resolving questions not committed to us by the Constitution, we may gain some public acclaim in the short run. In the long run, however, we will cease to be perceived as neutral arbiters, and we will lose that public respect so vital to our function."

10 Quoted in Deborah H. King, "Clara Shortridge Foltz: Angel and Revolutionary," 11 *Hastings Women's L. J.* 179 (2000).

11 Anthony Lewis, "To Realize Gideon: Competent Counsel with Adequate Resources," *The Champion*, March 1998.

12 Fred R. Shapiro, *Oxford Dictionary of Legal Quotations* (1993).

Stimson Bullitt

May 24, 2000

IT IS A PLEASURE TO BE HERE, BUT I FEEL AS IF I have been asked to describe the Cascade Mountains in five minutes without talking too fast. Stimson Bullitt is a big subject,[1] and he has his own cliffs, meadows, snowfields, towering peaks, and occasional rockslides. But I will try to give an overview.

There are, first of all, Stim's achievements as a builder and shaper of this city. Business was not his natural calling. His friend Bagley Wright says: "Stimson Bullitt was the first person I met when I came west from New York. We soon discovered that we admired the novels of Henry James and decided on the basis of this common interest to go into the real estate business together." Yet Stim has changed the face and heart of Seattle for the better. He envisioned Harbor Steps, struggled through years of difficulties, and brought it into existence. It is a magnificent gift to the city—an outdoor staircase designed by the renowned architect Arthur Erickson, and a complex of office and residential towers.[2]

For years the company Stim headed acquired rundown properties along Western and First Avenues. These were transformed into about 1,300 good residential units—many of them available at modest rentals.

Then there is his philanthropy. No one has done a better job of overcoming the handicap of having been born into a wealthy and prominent family. As Stim puts it, one of his goals has been "to rise from the rich." In his memoir, he dismisses his own philanthropy with a single sentence: "Over the years, most of my worldly goods have been given away." But his contributions to the environment, to civil rights, and to other worthy causes have been not just generous but exemplary.

The visible parts of Stim's legacy bring to mind a message on display in St. Paul's Cathedral in London. It was written about the great architect Christopher Wren, and it says: "If you seek his monument, look around you." (It's actually written in Latin but I will spare you my pronunciation.)

There is much more. As president of KING Broadcasting, Stim ran a television and radio company that set a national standard for excellence. In 1966, before the Vietnam War became unpopular, he appeared on camera himself to speak against it. Those editorials took both insight and courage.

The KING years were one chapter in a lifetime of civic commitment. In 1942, Stim wrote to members of Congress in defense of Japanese Americans. He has worked tirelessly to end racial discrimination. He has served on the King County Charter Commission. He has been honored by the creation of the Stimson Bullitt Professorship in Environmental Law at the University of Washington Law School.

Stim has given us another rare gift. He has written books that shine like diamonds amid the muddy ooze of most contemporary prose. The first one, a reflection on public life entitled *To Be a Politician*,[3] was reviewed nationally as "brilliant and original," "a small political classic," "a soaring work of the moral imagination," and "a masterpiece." His more recent book, *River Dark and Bright*, is a candid, moving, and enlightening memoir.[4]

These books are full not just of wisdom but of aphorisms, some of which will end up in Bartlett's Familiar Quotations. For example:

"He who wishes to excel as a lawyer should forswear politics."

"A politician may be lonely but he cannot be alone."

"Life may be meaningless, but politics is not."

And one that I can especially relate to: "Lawyers are not compelled to retire. They are allowed to dwindle."

And there is still more. A great citizen leads not just by achievements but by the example of his or her character. Stim would agree with the ancient Roman who said that "every man is the architect of his own fate," and he practices his own architecture with an insatiable desire not for applause but for merit and virtue.

Of course, not every effort succeeds. He writes: "After some years of taking cold showers upon rising as a means to improve my character . . . the effort appearing to have been made without avail, I abandoned the practice."

Stim is an athlete—formerly a boxer and now a ski racer and mountain climber and ocean sailor. He insists that he does not like danger; if that is true, danger must be unduly fond of him, because on five occasions he has come out of the mountains with broken bones, and several other times he has escaped death through what appears to be divine intervention.

He is a philosopher. In 1944 he carried a copy of Montaigne's essays ashore in the invasion of Leyte. He is fond of quoting the likes of Marcus Aurelius. If he owned a sports team they would undoubtedly be called the Seattle Stoics.

He is great conversationalist. We all know there are two kinds of conversationalists: the few who are wise enough to listen to what *we* have to say, and the many who want only to subject us to what *they* have to say. Stim listens, and he is genuinely modest. To give you one example, he and I have had long and enjoyable talks and, among many other subjects, have touched upon that of military service. I have not hesitated to speak of my adventures as a JAG officer in occupied Germany, when no shots were being fired in anger. Stim, under questioning, has told me something about his time in the South Pacific in World War II, when plenty of shots were being fired. But, typically of him, he never has mentioned that he volunteered for a landing party in the Philippines, was wounded by shrapnel, and still carries a piece of it in his shoulder.

Many friends and acquaintances have gotten the impression that Stim Bullitt is a visitor from another time and place—that he is here because of a time warp. He has been traced to ancient Athens, ancient Rome, the Florence of the Medicis, and sixteenth-century France. These attributions are incorrect and fail to credit Stim for being the modern person that he is. He is actually a man of the *eighteenth* century. With his devotion to the classics, his faith in knowledge and reason, his belief in democracy and in the virtues of citizenship, he needs only knee breeches and a wig to fit into that famous group portrait of the 1787 constitutional convention.

The late historian of ideas Isaiah Berlin wrote that the "intellectual power, honesty, lucidity, courage, and disinterested love of the most gifted thinkers of the eighteenth century remain to this day without parallel."5 But there is a parallel here in Seattle, to our good fortune.

If I may be permitted one more reference to architecture, it is said of Frank Lloyd Wright that his most productive years were between the ages of seventy and ninety. Stim is in better shape than Mr. Wright was, and from him it is fair to expect great things between the ages of eighty and one hundred. In the meantime, the Seattle-King County Association of Realtors has rightly designated as First Citizen a great friend not just to those who know him best but to our city, state, and nation, and indeed to the whole shrinking world—Stimson Bullitt.

1 Stimson Bullitt, a gifted Seattle lawyer and businessman, has broad experience in politics on local, state, and national levels. A ninth-generation American lawyer, he practiced until very recently, after graduating from the University of Washington School of Law in 1948. Beginning in the 1950s, immersed in politics, he was a delegate to Democratic conventions, was elected to the county charter-drafting commission, and lost two races for Congress. Through the 1960s, he headed a company that operated television and radio stations and other media outlets. His interests, as his memoir, *River Dark and Bright*, shows, are very broad and include government reorganization, political process reforms, race relations, and conservation.

2 Bagley Wright, often called Seattle's "patron saint of the arts," was a developer of the landmark Space Needle and chairman of Physio Control Corporation from 1968 until its acquisition by Eli Lilly in 1980. He and his wife, Virginia, began a collection of modern and contemporary art that is widely recognized as one of the most outstanding in the nation. Wright also served as founding president of the Seattle Repertory Company, which later honored him by naming its theater for him.

Arthur Erickson, the renowned Canadian architect, was a key figure in the design of Harbor Steps, part of which is a park (Seattle's version of Rome's Spanish steps) that connects First and Western avenues with a series of cascading plazas marked with enough generous landings to make it an enjoyable ascent and with enough downward trickling water which helps mask the traffic sounds.

3 Bullitt, *To Be a Politician* (New York: Doubleday, 1959; reprinted by Yale University Press, 1977).

4 Bullitt, *River Dark and Bright* (Seattle: Willows Press, 1995).

5 Quoted in Edward O. Wilson, "Back From Chaos," *The Atlantic Monthly*, March 1998, vol. 281, p. 41, n. 3.

Remembering Chuck Goldmark

GOLDMARK AWARD LUNCHEON

LEGAL FOUNDATION OF WASHINGTON

February 23, 2001

JUST OVER FIFTEEN YEARS AGO—IN DECEMBER 1985—my wife and I were invited to Christmas Eve dinner at the home of our friends Chuck and Annie Goldmark.[1] We had to decline with regret because we had visitors and had planned a gathering at our house. So instead of being at the Goldmarks' on Christmas Eve we were at home. That night came a telephone call from Peter Goldmark, Chuck's brother, with news so unwelcome that in memory I can still hear his voice on the telephone. And I spent the rest of that sleepless night, and the next day, along with a growing number of other friends, at Harborview Hospital, talking with the police, hanging onto every word we could get from the overworked doctors and nurses, hoping for favorable reports that never came.

We all know that calamities are part of life, but this one was exceptional. Chuck Goldmark and his beautiful wife, Annie, were among the best our very uneven species can produce. He was a skilled, coura-

geous, and public-spirited lawyer and, among many other achievements, an accomplished mountaineer. (A photograph taken by Stim
Bullitt in the Cascades in 1982 shows the three of us. We had been
hiking and had just stopped for the night on a rocky ledge; Chuck is
gazing upward toward where we would go the next day; I am sitting
down and probably asking when the cocktail hour would begin.)
Annie was a gifted linguist, a charming companion, and a loving
mother. Their two children, Derek and Colin, were bilingual, bright, and
promising—but above all, they were just young boys.

All four of them were cherished by a large and diverse group of
friends, and when their lives were taken so brutally, so senselessly,
so profoundly in violation of the most elemental standards of law
and morals, it seemed that fate was not just being arbitrary, as it often
is, but was determined to mock every virtue and destroy every hope.

There was an immense outpouring of anger and grief—and then,
after the first shock had passed, a new consensus. All of us at once,
so it seemed, decided that the legacy of Christmas Eve, 1985, would
be not despair but action, not resignation but a resolve to pick up the
torch, to honor Chuck and his family by bringing their ideals into
reality as well as we could.

That flame is still burning, and one expression of it is the annual
Goldmark Award Luncheon. Chuck would be pleased that this event
is held in his memory, and doubly pleased that today we will honor
Ken MacDonald and hear from Bob Utter—two of the finest cham-
pions of justice in the history of our state.[2]

Any description of Chuck Goldmark as a person must begin at a
sprawling, isolated wheat and cattle ranch in Eastern Washington.
He and Peter grew up there in the company of two remarkable parents, John and Sally. Nature is often rough, winter and summer, in
that part of the country, and the boys were always close to nature.
As Chuck said later, "By giving us life on the ranch, John and Sally
gave us something very special—the chance to learn things that few
people ever learn. How a cow reacts to a cutting horse. What the grass

is like in the spring. What the wind sounds like in a blizzard. We were in a place where your life was what you made it. No one else was in control. No one else was able to decide whether you could make it through the next day."

The boys picked rocks from the fields, ran farm machinery, planted and threshed wheat, herded cattle. They went to a one-room country school on the Indian reservation, and later to high school in town.

Chuck was a teenage boy when I first got to know him. He was already a capable ranch hand, and, in the years that followed, he became an airplane pilot, college student, international student leader, Army officer, law student, husband and father, and lawyer.

As a grown man, he was physically strong and tireless, and even mountain climbing came naturally to him. His partner Jim Wickwire, who knows what he's talking about, says that Chuck quickly became very good at mountaineering without ever making a full commitment to it.

He did make a full commitment to his wife and children. As Peter says, "Chuck devoted himself to his family and had the unique ability to leave work and reenter family life with energy and tremendous enthusiasm. He played constantly with the children at activities they loved: electronics, books, puzzles, skiing, hiking, biking, and rocketry. . . . And if Annie needed Chuck for support, he immediately dropped everything to be there."

As a lawyer, Chuck was brilliant and clear minded, hard working and well spoken, cool under pressure, and unfailingly kind and generous. He brought out the best in everyone who worked with him— usually just by his example but sometimes by exhortation. Barbara Clark recalls that Chuck was her first contact when she was hired to establish the Legal Foundation in 1984. She says: "I lived in Lynnwood at the time and on my first day of work there was a major snowstorm. I called Chuck to say I didn't think I could make it in. In a matter-of-fact manner he indicated that I could make it; I just needed to apply myself with a little more energy to the problem. And, of course, I did make it."[3]

Above all, Chuck knew what being a lawyer should mean. He knew that just as the composer's job is to create music (he was a great fan of Bach), and the artist's job is to create beauty, the lawyer's calling is to create justice. As Kevin Kelly has said, "Chuck believed that it is the responsibility of each of us . . . to try to improve some aspect of society beyond ourselves."[4] He served that ideal with an ever growing confidence, ability, and success, and without caring who got the credit.

I remember a remark made by the president of the Washington State Bar Association in the early 1980s. Chuck had just argued before the State Supreme Court in support of the IOLTA plan that would make millions of dollars in unused interest on lawyer's trust accounts available for legal aid to the poor.[5] The bar president did not know Chuck very well, but he was present for the hearing. He said afterward that hearing Goldmark argue that day had made him proud to be a lawyer.

Chuck was a co-founder of the Washington Legal Foundation, and he became its president. There were other causes—the North Slope Eskimos and the Pike Place Market, among others—which he served with the highest distinction.

At forty-one years of age, Chuck was in his early prime. Given a normal life span, he would have accomplished much more for our community and our nation—but it was not to be.

Well, these few words are only a sketch, and we cannot bring back our friend and colleague. What we can do is to carry on the work he would have done had he lived, and in that way to give him and his family the one kind of immortality that is within our power to confer. When we do that, we can be sure that if Chuck were here he would say: "Way to go. Today you gave it all you had. That's good enough. But tomorrow, with a little more energy, you can do better."

Thank you.

1 Charles A. Goldmark was a prominent Seattle attorney who played a very important part in the creation of the Interest on Lawyers' Trust Accounts (IOLTA) program. Mr. Goldmark was president of the Legal Foundation of Washington at the time he and his family were murdered in December 1985.

2 A 1942 graduate of Harvard Law School, Ken MacDonald has engaged in the general practice of law since 1949, with an emphasis on employment law. He served as chair of the Washington State Human Rights Commission from 1962 to 1968. He is a past president and board member of the American Civil Liberties Commission of Washington and has taught regularly at Seattle University School of Law. Robert F. Utter served on the Washington State Supreme Court from 1971 to 1995, and as Chief Justice from 1979 to 1981. A graduate of the University of Washington School of Law in 1954, Justice Utter served as a deputy prosecuting attorney and court commissioner, as well as on both the King County Superior Court and the Washington State Court of Appeals before joining the State Supreme Court.

3 Barbara Clark, a graduate of the University of Puget Sound School of Law, was Executive Director of the Legal Foundation of Washington at the time of the speech.

4 Kevin Kelly is past president of the Legal Foundation of Washington and a shareholder of Heller Ehrman, LLP.

5 IOLTA stands for Interest on Lawyers' Trust Accounts, which are, pursuant to the plan, paid to charitable or law-related purposes, such as providing legal aid to the poor. The concept originated in the 1960s in Australia and Canada. The first IOLTA program began in Florida in 1978. Using IOLTA funds, the State Supreme Court of Washington created the Legal Foundation of Washington in 1984. By 1995, all fifty states and the District of Columbia had IOLTA programs.

Emmett Watson Memorial

May 21, 2001

Emmett Watson and I were friends for about forty years. He watched parts of a few trials when I was a practicing lawyer—he was a great believer in the possibility of justice—but most of our time together was spent in other settings: in bars and restaurants, baseball u-bat-ems, small airplanes with him at the controls, tennis courts (believe it or not), or just walking around the city. He was an original, 1930s–40s Seattle man who never really changed and seemed immune to the charms of power, wealth, prestige, and all the rest. [1] He couldn't remember that he was famous. He was deeply devoted to his own bad habits (smoking, drinking, consumer debt, and sloth). His heart never moved from where he had started—among the working people, the poor, the longshoremen, the stump farmers, the dispossessed. He was a quiet man, always listening, and not just because he was hard of hearing; he listened because he wanted to know what you had to say.

He began in sports and moved on to the larger field of life in general, and he wrote with such insight, grace, and humor that he became one of the nation's greatest columnists. He was never full of himself, and he was generous in praising other writers—if they were good. When the *New York Times* sports columnist Red Smith died,[2] Emmett wrote: "right up to the end [Smith] was a virtuoso who could reach the high notes."

That was true of Watson himself. Because he was so casual, self-effacing, and covered with cigarette ashes, while his prose flowed so musically, many thought his work was effortless. He was a natural, but his best work was not effortless; it came through single-minded concentration and was based on a solid knowledge of English prose, structure, and style. He even knew a lot about poetry. If you quoted a line of English poetry to him, he could tell you who wrote it—if it was really good, that is.

Emmett was also set apart from ordinary men by the strength and vigor of his enthusiasms. While many go through life in a state of torpid indifference, Watson caught fire. Photography, skiing, cooking—these and many other pursuits fleetingly engaged his interest, only to subside quickly, leaving behind discarded equipment in his basement and insolvency among the friends who witlessly joined his quest for new horizons.

Emmett had unsuspected reserves of energy and talent. In 1982, for a charity production of "Inherit the Wind," we cast him against type as Hornbeck, the cynical newspaperman based on H. L. Mencken. Emmett was terrific; at an early rehearsal he was so good in his big scene that our director, Ted d'Arms, broke into applause. We had an SRO run of eight performances, netted a profit for the cause, and had a lot of fun. The stars were Murray Guterson, Jack Dutt, and that veteran but never cynical newspaperman, Emmett Watson.[3]

In 1988, at his seventieth birthday party, I gave a talk that included something like this: "We often celebrate Emmett's birthday. Why? Is it because he is a great writer and we all hope to have him do our obituaries (put in the file years in advance, of course)? No, it isn't that. We know other great writers and we do not celebrate their birthdays.

"Is it because he is an intrepid reporter who gets scoops? Such as that famous national scoop about Ernest Hemingway's last day? It's not that either.

"Is it because of his skill as a political leader—the founder of Lesser Seattle, whose membership is entirely fictitious? No. Other leaders' birthdays go unremembered.

"Is it because he is a fearless airplane pilot—one of the few surviving pilots who is both deaf and absent-minded? It can't be that.

"Is it, perhaps, due to his prowess in sports? He has been known to ski down almost-vertical slopes, although whether this was intentional is unclear. And he was a professional baseball player with a lifetime batting average of .500—one bloop single in two at-bats. But athletic ability cannot be the explanation.

"Could it be our surprise and delight, knowing of Emmett's airy contempt for everything the doctor orders, at finding him still with us each year? No, we have other friends who look even worse, and we do not celebrate their birthdays.

"I will tell you what it is. Emmett has seen a lot and done a lot. He knows the insides of bars, prizefighters' gyms, pool halls, and police stations. He has rubbed against the sleazy side of politics. He has fathomed the souls of tycoons. He has even fallen into some power himself, but in a way, none of it has ever touched him. His heart may be hooked up to three or four plastic devices, but it is pure. He makes us laugh, yet he always speaks to the best that is in us. And he is—in spite of everything, and after all these years—an innocent man."

Once in a while, when Emmett's indignation was fired up, he would take on a cause. He did this without ever tooting his own horn, which made his prose all the more effective, and without fear. He was an early opponent of the Vietnam War, an early critic of law-breaking by the Nixon administration, an objector to any desecration of the

Pike Place Market, and a droll critic of what is generally called "development." Seattle, he wrote, is

> a city that long ago became too big for its bridges, but still, somehow, retains a small-town character. Going big league in sports and restaurants, opera and theatre, yet definitely cut of the mainstream of dizzying fads and fashions; for the most part liberal and tolerant of neighbors and offbeat lifestyles. Maybe, when the world ends, Seattle will still have one more year to go.[4]

That was in 1979. Since then all efforts to keep us out of the mainstream have failed, but Emmett took these defeats in good spirits.

This spring, while going through medical miseries, our friend did not change. He did not become sentimental and he kept his powers of observation and his sense of humor. When I visited him in the hospital one day in April, he couldn't talk but was able to listen and write notes in response. I mentioned that I had given up cigarettes thirty-seven years ago. Emmett wrote: "I gave them up four weeks ago." I told him I was about to begin chemotherapy. Emmett absorbed this news for a minute and wrote: "Why don't you get your chemo started by having a drink?"

There will never be another Emmett Watson, or even a facsimile. Seattle won't be the same. But luckily, he left us plenty of words to remember him by.

NOTES

1 Emmett Watson, 1918–2001, was a fixture of Seattle journalism for more than fifty years. He started as a sportswriter for the *Seattle Star* and then became a columnist for the *Seattle Post-Intelligencer* and the *Seattle Times*. Although sports, mainly baseball, was his major interest, social commentary crept into his columns over the years. He was a champion of civil

rights, social reform and the anti-war movement. He regularly targeted the self-righteous guardians of public morality. To separate himself from growth booster types, he named himself press secretary for Lesser Seattle. He wrote and compiled several books, notably *Disgressions of a Native Son*.

2 Red Smith (1905–82) was an American sports columnist whose literary craftsmanship, deep knowledge of sports, and sense of humor made him one of the most revered and popular sportswriters.

3 Murray Guterson was Bill Dwyer's long-time law partner.

4 "Homage to Seattle," *Seatte P-I*, Jan. 7, 1979.

The Future of Litigation

FIRST ANNUAL JUDICIAL APPRECIATION DINNER

SEATTLE-KING COUNTY BAR ASSOCIATION;

EAST KING COUNTY BAR ASSOCIATION;

SOUTH KING COUNTY BAR ASSOCIATION

February 24, 1987

•

HONORED JUDGES, MAYOR ROYER, COUNTY EXECUTIVE Hill, distinguished guests, ladies and gentlemen.[1] It is a great pleasure to be here this evening and especially to speak in honor of our judiciary.

Several of my old friends, an outspoken lot, have asked how it came about that I was asked to address this gathering. The answer is, I don't know. But you can see what the committee must have been up against. They could have gotten Howard Cosell, but his fee for an event like this is about $15,000. Emmett Watson charges a fee too, maybe a little bit less, and besides that, his legal views are so heavily biased in favor of freedom of the press as to make him of doubtful utility at an occasion like this. On the other hand, my speaker's fee happens to be zero, for reasons that I hope will not become too obvious, and my travel expenses are zero.

But, of course, I was deeply honored by the invitation, notwithstanding its obvious fiscal overtones, and to the treasurer's great relief I decided to accept it.

It was an irresistible invitation, after all, because the subject could be anything related to the law. So I decided to talk about the future of litigation.

Please do not assume from that title that I think I have all the answers. In fact, it became clear very early in my practice that I do not have all the answers. Years ago I was defending a criminal case in which my client was charged with having embezzled money from his company. It was claimed that he had done this by sending checks drawn on the company account to a business acquaintance in another city who would deposit the checks to his own account and then issue his checks to pay my client's personal bills here in Seattle. Now, to acquaint our client with what could happen if he took the witness stand in his own defense, we put him through a sample cross-examination. I played the role of the prosecutor, and the dry-run cross-examination went something like this:

"You say that you frequently sent checks drawn on your company's account to your friend Joe Doaks in Minneapolis?"
"Yes."

"You've seen from the evidence here that Mr. Doaks deposited those checks to his account in Minneapolis?"
"Yes."

"Then he paid your bills here in Seattle with checks drawn on his account?"
"Yes."

"For example, he paid your tailor's bill frequently that way?"
"Yes."

"Your gardener?"
"Yes."

"Other bills?"

"Yes."

"How was it, if you can tell the jury, that Mr. Doaks in Minneapolis was paying your bills here in Seattle?"

"It was more convenient to do it that way."

"With Doaks hundreds of miles away, and you in Seattle, and all the creditors in Seattle, how could that be a convenient way to pay the bills?"

"That's what I hired you guys to figure out!"

But recognizing that we do not have all the answers, let us turn tonight to a momentous question: How will the legal profession cope with one of the most difficult problems that our system of justice has ever faced: the overburdening of our courts with too many cases, and the resulting delay, expense, frustration, and injustice for citizens who need to get their disputes resolved in court?

We all know that we are blessed with a great system. We have constitutional liberty, trial by jury, an independent judiciary, and, in my opinion, the best and fairest system of dispute resolution in the world.

But in recent years the volume of cases, civil and criminal, confronting our courts has far outstripped the growth of the courts themselves. This has happened at such a rapid rate that we now have court congestion of a very serious kind.

Today 71 percent of the lawyers in the United States say that there is a serious backlog of civil cases in their jurisdictions. In the West the figure is 81 percent. The average delay in big cities around the country is about two years for a civil case, and in some cities it is more like four years from filing to trial.

In Chicago, a man ran a newspaper ad recently, saying that his divorce case had been pending in the Illinois courts for eight years and asking others to write to him if they were in a similar predicament. He got about a hundred replies.

In Philadelphia, the municipal court is so badly jammed that there is talk of a breakdown in the administration of justice.

In King County, with an excellent bench and a cooperative bar, it now takes twenty-six months to get to trial in a civil jury case.

Why is all this happening? Because there are too many cases, and too many complicated cases.

Court congestion, ladies and gentlemen, is not a mere inconvenience. It is a threat to the life of our system. Serious delay means expense, emotional strain for the parties, and injustice. It means that our system is not working as it should.

At the same time that we are suffering this degree of court congestion we also hear many complaints that our system is too contentious, that it involves too much dispute, that matters go on too long, and that it is too expensive. In fact, to take a civil case through the court system is simply beyond the means of many citizens.

These problems are appearing even in the best-run and best-administered big city jurisdictions.

What will happen? We will undoubtedly get more courts. We need them in many places. We need them right here. I believe we will get them in King County—more courts and more judges. But here and elsewhere, more courts and more judges can only be a partial answer to the problem. Beyond that, we need to make adjustments within the system. And the lead must be taken by us as lawyers and judges.

This is our great challenge: how to preserve our system, and preserve every litigant's right to a trial, but at the same time improve and simplify our procedures and create alternatives for our citizens so that the right to have a trial is exercised less often. It is a hard job and it will call on the best that we have to give it. But I believe that our profession will rise to the occasion.

Now for some predictions of changes that I think are likely to come about during, let's say, the balance of the twentieth century. Prediction is, of course, a risky business. But if anyone in the twenty-first century happens to read from the dusty files an account of this talk tonight, and if these predictions look ridiculous, please remember that Howard Cosell would have cost $15,000 and Emmett Watson would have insisted on talking about the First Amendment.

First, I think that promoting agreement is now becoming, and will become even more, an open and conscious objective of the courts. We have the adversary system in which the two sides hire lawyers, square off, dig up evidence, and present their cases against each other. It amounts to a kind of civilized battle. The right to do this, to have an adversary trial, is priceless and we must preserve it.

But we should also recognize that today in the United States trial is not the typical way of resolving disputes through litigation. The typical way is settlement. Most cases are settled. Most civil cases settle through an agreement. Most criminal cases settle through a negotiated plea of guilty. We need now to increase that measure of settlement in order to alleviate court congestion.

Traditionally, settlement is a kind of accidental by-product of the litigation process. Often it has been felt to involve a certain loss of face. Often settlements have occurred late in the day and after too much money has been spent.

Courts have traditionally favored settlements but have lacked any systematic means of bringing them about. That is now changing, and settlement is becoming a prime objective of the civil courts from the start of each case. We are using settlement judges; we are using volunteer lawyers as mediators. In this federal district the local rule that permits the judge to order the parties into mediation, with an uncompensated lawyer as mediator, has worked well and has become an example for other jurisdictions. More cases will settle in the future, I believe, and they will settle earlier and with more conscious participation by the court and by the bar, often with members of the bar working as unpaid volunteers.

The full significance of this change is just beginning to come into view. It is not just that mediation will help to alleviate court congestion, although that is important. What we are coming to, I believe, is a revised view of litigation in which litigants will come to court expecting not just the traditional battle, glorious though it may be, but expecting also to receive expert help in arriving at an agreement that will end the dispute.

Along a parallel track is alternative dispute resolution. This is a movement on which George Revelle and others in this room have worked a great deal and in which neighborhood centers are set up where people with disputes can try to resolve them with skilled help without resorting to litigation.[2]

With this trend toward promoting agreement, will we become like Japan, where agreement is the order of the day and litigation is rare? I don't think so. But we will surely be doing more and better things to bring about agreements.

Also, over the balance of this century, we will see more and more arbitration of small claims. We have that now in King County and it works very well. Arbitration, unlike mediation, is a kind of trial. It usually takes place outside the courthouse, and instead of a judge there is an arbitrator who, again, often is a practicing lawyer. Last year in King County more than 2,000 cases were removed from the court calendar through mandatory arbitration of small claims.

We will also see, I believe, over the next several years some shifting of the burden of the costs of litigation. We are all accustomed to the traditional American system in which each side bears its own attorney fees—win, lose, or draw—in most cases. The English have always had the opposite. In most civil cases in Great Britain the prevailing party wins an award of his or her attorney fees. Without getting into the merits of one philosophy versus the other, I believe that we will not adopt the English rule in its entirety, but will start awarding attorney fees in more situations than we have in the past.

We have an example now under the King County arbitration rule. If a party arbitrates a case and then insists on retrying it and fails to improve his position, the other side recovers attorney fees. Somebody in the next few years is bound to propose a mediation rule or statute under which the two sides must go before a mediator and try to reach agreement with the mediator's help; and if the mediator makes a final recommendation that one side rejects and the other side accepts, the rejecting side then proceeds to trial at the risk of incurring an award of attorney fees if that side fails to improve its position at trial. To the best of my knowledge that rule has not been proposed yet, but it is safe to expect that it will be put forward and will be debated vigorously.

And we will also start awarding attorney fees more often to prevailing parties where the other party's claim or defense has been asserted unreasonably and without reasonable cause. To that degree we will see a shifting of the burden of the costs of litigation.

We can also expect a widespread improvement in the handling of major cases. Major commercial cases can take a colossal and disproportionate amount of judicial time and resources.

Several years ago, I believe it was in 1978, our firm started a case for some cattle feeders against several meat packers. These were Eastern Washington cattle feeders, and they claimed antitrust violations by the meat packers. We decided to sue in state court because we thought we could get to trial sooner that way. We knew that in Texas, in federal court, there was then pending a multi-district class action for cattle feeders against meat packers, and we thought that if we filed in federal court we might get what they call 'multi-districted," transferred to Texas, and then get tangled up in a big class action. So we sued in state court. The case was assigned to Judge Elston and proceeded along briskly. The pretrial work was done, a trial date was set, and the case ended up being settled, I believe in 1980, to the reasonable satisfaction of all concerned. I think everyone on both sides would agree it was done expeditiously. And what happened in the meantime in the federal court class action in Texas? It was filed in 1976. In 1986, ten years later, an order was entered decertifying the class.

What that means is that very little happened in a decade except a massive expenditure of time, effort, and attorney fees. And without blaming anyone, the fact is that the bench and bar in Texas would surely agree with us that that kind of case history could be improved upon. I believe that it will be, and that the management of major litigation will be improved throughout the country.

Another development we can look forward to is that discovery will be brought under control. All the lawyers in the room know that discovery means depositions, production of documents, answering written interrogatories. Historically, discovery came into our system to do away with trial by ambush. I must say, I liked trial by ambush pretty well. It did have its moments. I remember one many years ago when I was defending a case as co-counsel with the late, great Charles Burdell Sr., whom many of you remember.[3] We had a tough assignment on our hands. It got all the tougher when a surprise witness was called by the prosecution. The surprise witness took the stand and started to give unexpected and very damaging evidence. And while this devastating testimony was coming in, I turned to Charlie at the counsel table and whispered, "What do we do now?" And he said, "Knock over the water pitcher." Something was lost when we lost trial by ambush.

Discovery is very valuable but it has been greatly overdone in many cases, often taking thousands of lawyer hours in a single case and resulting in massive expense and in a kind of paper war where the two sides submit stacks of papers, and argue about them, rather than really trying the case. I don't like those big stacks of paper. They take us too close to the inquisitorial system of some countries in which cases are decided primarily on the papers, and away from our system which is based on live testimony, cross-examination, the right of confrontation, and the adversary trial process.

Discovery abuses must and will be cut down and the process simplified. The American system will choose trial or settlement rather than paper wars.

Jury empanelments, I think, will also be simplified and shortened in those jurisdictions that have suffered from prolonged empanelments. Our state has been quite fortunate in that respect, but in some other parts of the country, we've seen the spectacle of weeks being taken to empanel a jury. The system cannot afford that and the public is rightly offended by it. In most cases, even complex cases, a day or less should be enough. And we can expect that the question will be put to us as practicing lawyers pretty soon: Do we want to continue the present system or do we want to accept time limits on questioning prospective jurors? Do we want, perhaps, to accept the federal system in which the judge does all of the preliminary questioning of the jurors? The bench and bar will probably be called upon to make that decision within the next few years.

There will be other steps taken toward brevity.

Briefs will be brief. Page limits will be enforced.

Trial time in some cases will be rationed. That is a step most trial lawyers would be loath to see and most judges would be reluctant to impose. But it is happening now in complex cases in various parts of the country, the judge saying that the burdens on the calendar are such that you have X number of days to try this case. Spend them as you wish. It takes great skill to do that without causing injustice. It is risky, but I believe we can expect that more of it will be happening.

Appellate courts will be writing, I believe, shorter decisions and perhaps fewer decisions, and deciding more cases via short memorandum decisions rather than with a fun opinion.

And, ladies and gentlemen, plain English will take over as the language of the legal profession. "Legalese" will pass out of the scene. Maybe even "Esquire" will fall into disuse. We might think for a moment how "Esquire" looks to somebody who is not called Esquire. A friend of mine has the idea of getting rid of all such, as she sees it, affectations, by awarding every man, woman, and child in the United States an honorary doctor of philosophy degree so that everyone would be entitled from birth to be called "Doctor."

We can look forward also to an increase in pro bono—free legal work for deserving causes and for impecunious clients. That is a great tradition of our profession, which will grow even stronger as we work toward our ideal of equal justice for all.

You will have noticed that there is nothing drastic in these predictions. No fundamental change is foreseen. That, I believe, is as it should be, because our basic job has always been to conserve what we have been lucky enough to inherit.

And of course these predictions are not exhaustive. Other things will happen that I haven't mentioned and haven't thought of. All I have tried to do is give you a few glimpses of what one lawyer sees as the future of litigation.

Will we succeed? We don't know yet.

But we do know that the United States Constitution gives us the best chance to succeed that any society could have. It was just two hundred years ago this week, in February 1787, that the call went out from the Continental Congress to the thirteen states to send delegates to Philadelphia to write a new constitution.

The most persuasive voice in bringing that about was that of a lawyer, Alexander Hamilton. Most of the delegates were lawyers. And in that hot summer in Philadelphia, they produced what the English statesman William E. Gladstone later referred to as "the most wonderful work ever struck off at a given time by the brain and purpose of man"—a government of limited powers, a careful separation of powers, a bill of rights, and, above all, a government based on law.

No other society has been so fortunate as ours in translating written rules of law into a genuine, everyday system of ordered liberty. Litigation in the courts, both criminal and civil, is a kind of lifeblood of that liberty.

That is why we are right to talk about ways of improving our court system even when the world is faced with grievous problems of fanaticism, war, overpopulation, and resource depletion. Those are massive problems indeed, but we know that law is the means of solving problems peaceably and honorably. And we agree with our nineteenth-century colleague Daniel Webster (Webster, by the way, was not only a great lawyer and senator but the champion eater of raw oysters in Massachusetts), who said, "Justice is the ligament which holds civilized beings and civilized nations together."[4]

And that is why it is especially fitting that we honor our judiciary tonight. As Alexander Hamilton said, "There is no liberty if the power of judging be not separated from the legislative and judicial powers."[5] That independent judiciary has been a foundation stone of our freedom for two centuries.

Since I am still entirely free to speak in praise of judges, it should be mentioned that when one becomes a judge he or she usually takes a loss of income, becomes committed to what seems to be an endless flow of difficult work, gives up the God-given right to stay out of the news, has to dress in black, and, maybe most serious of all for lawyers, has to let somebody else do most of the talking.

We are fortunate in Washington State to have a bench—federal, state, and local—that is capable, hard-working, honest, and fair.

So, on behalf of the bar, and, if I may, on behalf of the community, I thank our honored guests tonight for their service and their dedication. And let all of us, lawyers and other citizens, join our judges in seeking the truth, serving our Constitution, and strengthening the courthouse as the house of justice.

NOTES

1 Charles Royer served three terms as mayor of the City of Seattle, from 1978 to 1990. Tim Hill served two terms as King Country Executive, from 1986 to 1993.

2 George H. Revelle Jr. (1913–99) was a distinguished King County Superior Court judge, a respected attorney, a colonel in the U.S. Army during World War II, and, in Seattle, a well-known churchman at St. Mark's Episcopal Cathedral.

3 Charles Burdell, Sr. (1912–73) was a well-known Seattle lawyer with Ferguson and Burdell, with whom Dwyer, in private practice, worked as co-counsel.

4 The quotes from Gladstone and Webster are from Fred R. Shapiro's *Oxford Dictionary of American Legal Quotations* (1993).

5 From *The Federalist*, no. 78, p. 523 (Cooke edition, 1961), quoting Montesquieu, "The Spirit of Laws."

Rumpole Was Right

HOW THE WORLD LOOKS TO A FEDERAL JUDGE, AND

HOW THE AMERICAN LEGAL SYSTEM WILL BE SAVED

THE MONDAY CLUB

April 30, 199

I HAD MEANT TO DO A LOT OF ORIGINAL RESEARCH for my first Monday Club paper[1] and to present to you, my fellow members, an essay on something like Spain's Future in the Common Market, or New Hope in the Battle against Aphids. But then, at one of our recent meetings, Bob Heilman said: "I hope you'll give us a paper soon on How the World Looks to a Federal Judge. I've always wondered how the world looks to somebody who sees it passing through a courtroom."[2] This of course was an irresistible invitation. I am going to speak on Professor Heilman's subject. I will also throw in, at no extra charge, a few words about how the American legal system will be saved. During this talk, I will quote others and will mention work that others are doing. It must be understood that the persons I quote or refer to are not responsible for any defects in this paper. No, in all candor, I must admit that any shortcomings in what I am about to say are entirely the responsibility of Bob Heilman.

I have now been a judge for two years and five months. Before that I was a trial lawyer for thirty-three years, counting three years in the army and three decades in private practice. I had worked in many trials and negotiations and other contests before my present job came along, and I was accustomed to seeing the world as it appears in raw wars.

But there is a new vantage point starting the day you become a judge. You find yourself wearing a black robe. Everybody calls you "Your Honor." You sit above the fray at an elevated bench. Your utterances descend as if by the force of gravity to the lower regions of the courtroom. You may have had a lifetime of difficulty in getting people's attention—you may still be unable to get a word in at home or to catch a waiter's eye in restaurants—but now, when you speak, all present stop and listen. Many actually take notes of what you are saying.

It is remarkable how quickly one can get used to this kind of treatment. Do you remember the old movies in which a beggar who happens to look like the king is installed temporarily in his place for reasons of state convenience? In no time the man from the streets figures that wearing ermine and being called "Your Majesty" are only his rightful due. And so it is with a trial judge newly appointed from the ranks of the hardworking and competitive private bar.

To save himself from a fatal delusion of grandeur—or "federalitis," as it is sometimes called—a judge needs to remember that all of this is an invitation to say less rather than more. The robe, the bench, the bang of the bailiff's gavel, the call "All rise!" are intended not to recognize natural merit but to compensate for its absence. The best judges may have less fun than some of the worst ones, but they have no illusions; they know that the trappings of office merely give weight to rulings which might be less persuasive if announced in a business suit at floor level.

Once off the bench at the end of the day, it is gratifying to find that one's anonymity has survived almost completely intact. I can

walk for miles through the city without being recognized by anyone but old friends. Many people, on hearing what I do for a living,
assume that I work in Washington, D.C. It is necessary to explain
that there are about 760 federal judges in the country, counting the
Supreme Court, the courts of appeal, and the district courts; that these
760 preserve and enforce the Constitution and federal laws for a
nation of 250 million people; that the district judges, who make up
over 500 of the total, are the federal trial judges and serve in their
home states; and that the district judges try federal criminal cases,
civil cases brought under federal law, and civil cases brought under
state law where the parties are citizens of different states. By the
time this has been explained, the average person's attention span
has been exhausted and anonymity returns.

The work is demanding, satisfying, and always interesting. Even
the cases that look boring at the beginning turn out to be interesting once you get into them. Nearly always, anyway. And there is the
gratifying knowledge that if you do the job right you can make a difference for the better in many lives, and can add a few bricks and a
little mortar to the great house of the law.

There is also the pleasure of working with lawyers. I like lawyers.
I like to watch their good work. I feel for them in their misfortunes.
And I enjoy it when they are funny without meaning to be, as even
the best ones sometimes are.

Here is a verbatim excerpt from a final argument made to me in
a bench trial (a case tried to the court without a jury):

"Now, Your Honor, I would like to put a red herring to bed." I
refrained from saying: "Every man to his own taste."

Here is a passage from another closing argument by a lawyer, this
time to a jury: "Ladies and gentlemen, there are three kinds of lies:
lies, damned lies, and statistics." Then the same lawyer, same argument, ten minutes later: "Ladies and gentlemen, look at the numbers. The numbers don't lie!" Maybe they don't, but jurors do
remember what they are told from one minute to the next.

I must say also that working with my fellow judges and magistrates has been a great pleasure. In some districts—not in the Pacific Northwest—federal judges have feuds and quarrels. Not so in Western Washington. We are a congenial group of seven active judges, one senior judge, and three full-time magistrates.

Criminal cases must be tried first, by act of Congress, and they are certainly first in the hearts of our countrymen. As a young lawyer, I tried a lot of criminal cases and became deeply impressed with mankind's ability to invent an almost infinite variety of brutal, dishonest, or demented conduct. That impression has been fully confirmed in the past two and a half years.

There is no single criminal type, but there are many types. Many years ago the notorious bank jobber Willy Sutton, who had been to prison a few times, was asked why he kept on robbing banks. "Because that's where the money is," he answered. But there is more to bank robbery than that. Bank robbery is not just a way of laying hands on ready cash, but a mode of self-expression. For a brief moment the robber basks in the sunshine of power and influence, while everybody in sight obeys his orders. The people who commit this crime tend to be young or middle-aged, male, virile, and energetic. Some of them are proud of their craft. Some are polite. In one of my cases the crime was committed just before the winter holidays, and the robber, walking out with the cash, said to the teller, "Thank you, and have a merry Christmas." Many are careless. One who came before me for sentencing had been caught about two hours after the heist. In his pocket the police found not only the marked money but the note he had used and thoughtlessly kept, saying in his own handwriting: "I have a gun. Keep quiet and give me your cash." He didn't really have a gun, as most of them don't.

Then there are the embezzlers. Most of these, in federal court anyway, are women. Usually they have no previous record. Seeing a river of money pass before their eyes at the office, they have dipped into it. Many of them have worthless husbands, or none, or children to support. Many are emotionally ravaged just by being caught and prosecuted. They are hard to sentence. The late Don Voorhees, our fellow Monday Club member, hated these cases more than any others.[3]

And there are the drug dealers. These are a multitude, and among them we find all types: murderous gangsters, respectable business and professional people, addicts financing their habit, poor kids from Mexico trying to help out the folks back home. One woman I sentenced, a waitress from Hong Kong who had four children to support and a mah-jong debt to pay, had been talked by the Chinese mafia into flying to the United States with packets of heroin strapped to her body. She spoke only Chinese, she had no record, and she wept for her children—but the law required a long sentence in an American prison. (Lest you think that the phrase "Chinese mafia" is an ethnic oxymoron, I assure you that there are mafias all over. I have sentenced alleged members of the Hungarian mafia and the Nigerian mafia.)

My first major criminal case as a judge was the nation's first homicide trial under a federal statute that prohibits tampering with consumer products. You may remember that in the mid 1980s there was a brief wave of lethal tampering with over-the-counter capsules. Two people died in Auburn, Washington: a truck driver and, several days later, a young woman who managed a branch bank. It took a year and a half to crack the case with the help of brilliant work by the FBI laboratory in Washington. The defendant was the truck driver's wife. She had wanted double indemnity insurance proceeds and had placed cyanide in her husband's Excedrin capsules, thinking that the death would be blamed on an unknown product tamperer. When the coroner missed the diagnosis—emphysema, he said at first—she planted poisoned capsules in a jar on a store shelf, thinking that the death of another person would lead to a second autopsy of her husband and a corrected finding for insurance purposes. And so it did, after the death of the unfortunate woman who bought the second bottle. At the trial, the defendant's grown daughter testified against her, weeping copiously. The defendant took the stand in her own behalf and also wept copiously. Both were persuasive but the jury found the defendant guilty, mostly on circumstantial evidence. I sentenced her to ninety years in prison. *People* magazine ran a story on the case, with pictures. Then, while the defendant was in jail during the appeal, she got into a loud quarrel with a fellow inmate. As they parted company, she was heard to call out a warning to the other woman: "Remember where I work!" She was working, it seems, in the prison kitchen.

This spring I tried cases for two weeks in Tucson, Arizona, to help out a district that has far too many criminal cases for the few judges there. In one case, the defendant was an employee of the United States Forest Service, for which he had worked for many years. He was charged with arson—with deliberately setting a fire in the Coronado National Forest. The fire had raged out of control and finally been put out with the help of volunteer firefighters. The evidence again was circumstantial and the defendant did not testify. After a long deliberation the jury found him guilty. Why would he have done such a thing? He lived in a small town. His friends were members of the volunteer fire department. When a forest fire started he would be the first to report it. The volunteers would come and put it out, and would get paid by the government for their services. The defendant probably had set several fires over the years to help keep his fellow townsmen busy and prosperous.

I will give one more example of mankind's insatiable appetite for crime. This too was a case I tried last month in Tucson. The main defendant was a U.S. marshal—not only that, he was one of the highest ranking officers in the marshals' service. For two hundred years the marshals have had a proud tradition of safeguarding the federal judiciary and capturing fugitives from justice. This officer had been in charge of international operations; he had to his credit the tracking down of Josef Mengele, the Nazi war criminal, and other famous achievements. But he had gotten into a love affair with a young woman deputy marshal at Peoria, Illinois. And then he drew her into a pattern of picking up men in bars and having sex with them in her apartment or a hotel room, while he, the high-ranking marshal, listened and watched from the closet with a tape recorder running. From at least one of these men—a businessman from Kansas—the high ranking marshal then extorted money through anonymous phone calls and mailings. He was caught and convicted, and, of course, his law enforcement career, and hers, are ruined. As bizarre a case as you will ever see; psychiatrists can try to explain it, but with only limited success.

These cases I have told you about are not the run of the mill. The run of the mill these days is drugs—heroin, marijuana, methamphetamines, and, more than any of the others, cocaine. Seattle is a major port of entry for drugs from Thailand, Hong Kong, and Mexico. Domestically, we have supplies coming in steadily from California and the Yakima Valley in eastern Washington. We try, convict, and sentence a seemingly endless procession of drug dealers and couriers. Most federal judges feel they could try a cocaine case in their sleep.

Is our criminal justice system working?

In terms of convicting the guilty, acquitting the innocent, and protecting the rights of all concerned, the trial system is working very well. We do have fair trials. The rights enjoyed by any person accused of a crime—the presumption of innocence, the rights to trial by jury, to confront witnesses, to be represented by counsel (including counsel paid for by the government if the defendant is without means)—are unsurpassed anywhere in the world. On the whole, and certainly in this part of the country, we have the benefit of excellent work by the police, the prosecutors, and the defense bar.

Everything works well, ordinarily, through the process of arresting, charging, trying, and convicting. But then we slip several degrees in confidence and capability. Once the person is convicted, what next?

In serious cases our standard answer is prison, but we know it is a very unsatisfactory one. It is also a recent one in historical terms. It was only in the early nineteenth century that the widespread use of imprisonment as a punishment for crime began. Nowadays we rely on it too much. Today more than a million Americans are behind bars, counting about 750,000 in prisons and 300,000 in jails.

For many offenders, prison is the only answer, especially for repeaters who are no longer youthful. But we know that for many young people, who might be saved through the use of some imagination and close supervision, the result of a long term in prison may be the emergence of a hardened criminal.

Congress has made a difficult situation worse by requiring mandatory minimum sentences in some cases. We run into these most commonly in the field of drugs—a person convicted of possessing a certain amount of cocaine with the intent to distribute it, for example, may have to be sentenced to at least five or ten years in prison, regardless of his age, previous record, or the mitigating circumstances. These mandatory minimums take away the discretion that a sentencing judge needs to exercise in order to do justice. They are a step backward toward more primitive notions of justice, based on rigid categories of offense and retribution, such as those found in the Code of Hammurabi of about 1800 B.C. And in practice they cause injustice in many cases.

I will give you one example. A twenty-two-year-old man came before me having pleaded guilty to possessing cocaine with intent to distribute it. He was a member of a Los Angeles gang, but he did not have a serious prior record and had never been in prison. He was a low-ranking courier and had simply been caught at the airport with cocaine in his jacket pocket. A sentence to a year or two in prison, followed by a few years of supervised release, would have given him a strong punishment and a chance to recover. By act of Congress, I had to sentence him to at least ten years. He will have to serve about nine years of the ten. He will be past thirty when he gets out, and the result is not hard to imagine.

We have sentencing guidelines now which protect the public from unduly lenient sentences. The mandatory minimums are counter-productive and the idea of abolishing them is catching on. John Chancellor editorialized against them recently over the NBC television news. The Federal Courts Study Committee, appointed by Chief Justice William Rehnquist, calls for their abolition in its report published this month. Maybe Congress will listen.

Punishment for crime is a field we still don't understand very well. We need to be more imaginative, and we should be willing to learn from other societies. There are some new trends. In some parts of the country, young offenders are now sent to a kind of boot camp instead of jail. In Miami, some first-time offenders are turned over on probation to the Salvation Army; the results are reported to be good. In other parts of the world, productive work for prisoners, conjugal visits, and the use of day fines (payable as a remittance from the defendant's monthly earnings) are used with some success. As our prison population grows—and it is running ahead of our ability to house prisoners—we need more urgently than ever to make better use of community service, fines, and other alternatives.

The inevitable question to all judges and law enforcement officers is this: Do you think drugs should be legalized? It is true that law enforcement has not stopped the drug traffic. It is also true that the people we convict and sentence, by and large, rank low in the distribution hierarchy; many of them are so-called "mules" whose only function is to carry the stuff around for the bigger operators. Many of the biggest operators are not even in the United States and ply their trade from the relative safety of foreign countries. The traffic continues to flourish no matter how many people we lock up. Some judges feel like King Canute, shouting against the incoming tide.

But I do not believe that we should legalize drugs. If we do, we will be making highly addictive narcotics available to millions of our most vulnerable people, especially the poor and the children. We will be assuring an even larger number than we now get of babies born damaged or addicted. And we will be giving up the battle against drugs before it has really been fought.

The battle has not been fought in the sense that it never can be won through law enforcement alone. In the long run we must eliminate the demand—and that means we must have education, treatment, and a general lifting of the morale of society. We have done little about any of that except to put forth great clouds of rhetoric. We have not been willing to face the realities of a hard job or to spend the money or do the work to get it done. When we do become willing, the battle can be won.

Then there are the civil cases, to which most judges turn with a feeling of relief. These too have a wonderful variety: breach of contract, antitrust, personal injury, maritime accidents, securities fraud, environmental battles, and a host of others.

Saint Paul said in one of his letters to the Corinthians: "It is altogether a defect in you that you have lawsuits with one another."[4]

Napoleon, the sponsor of a groundbreaking legal code, said that lawsuits were "an absolute leprosy, a social cancer."

Ambrose Bierce, in *The Devil's Dictionary*, defined a lawsuit as "a machine which you go into as a pig and come out of as a sausage."[5]

And the famous Judge Learned Hand, who spent his life writing appellate court opinions, said that "as a litigant, I should dread a lawsuit beyond almost anything else short of sickness and death."[6]

Could they all have been wrong? According to the American public, yes. Civil litigation is pushing baseball as the national pastime. We have more cases, and more kinds of cases, than ever.

We should not be altogether dismayed by this. Litigation is one sign of the robustness of American Society—of our sense that legal rights are real, that each of us is an individual, that justice can be received by the weak against the strong. And it is important to remember that a civil trial is not just a matter of deciding who owes what to whom. It is also a kind of ritual and a way of restoring peace and reconciling conflicting values.

Those functions become more difficult as society becomes more specialized. Thomas Jefferson knew nearly everything there was to be known in the eighteenth century. Nobody remotely approaches that today. Few nonspecialists understand modern science and technology, and many specialists are deficient in politics, or in anything outside their line of work.

A pluralistic society must have a coherent center, where diverse values are understood and reconciled with the law. The complex commercial cases, the medical malpractice cases, and the patent infringement cases that we see are prime examples of this. To handle these well, the courts must understand what is going on in science, technology, and business.

Are the courts up to this kind of challenge? I believe they are—and that includes the juries.

I came into this job as a supporter of the jury system, and for that reason, I have cast a critical eye from this new vantage point on what juries do. Everything I have seen has strengthened my confidence. Juries do understand cases, even complex cases. They do justice. And they love their work—especially if a case is well tried.

Of all our democratic institutions, none works as well, day in and day out, as does the jury. And this strikes me as a great sign of hope for democracy. Think what might happen to the election process if the voters could decide based on the same quality of information they get in a courtroom after full and vigorous cross examination.

It seems to me that our civil trials, by and large, are fair and thorough and produce justice. Nowhere in the world do the litigants benefit from such a rigorous and careful examination of their claims and defenses.

But there are some things that we are not doing so well.

Civil litigation is too slow and too expensive. Many people are simply priced out of the court system.

Often I serve as a settlement judge, settling cases pending before other judges. Last year I mediated a case pending before a federal judge in Los Angeles. It was a construction case, a contractor suing a subcontractor, but the parties had thrown in a lot of other claims besides breach of contract: fraud, violation of the RICO statute,[7] and so on. The first question I asked the lawyers was this: How much is really at stake here if you measure it by the cost of the construction work that is in dispute? The answer was $1.75 million. The next question was: How much do the parties have in this case already (this was before trial) for attorney fees and costs? The answers added up to the same figure: $1.75 million.

A typical example of what can happen, unfortunately: too much contentiousness costing too many dollars.

The twin of growing expensiveness is delay in the courts: jammed dockets and years of waiting, especially in the big cities, with near-breakdowns of the civil justice system in Los Angeles, Houston, and a few other cities.

What can be done?

The key is that most civil cases don't get tried. Most are settled or dismissed. What has happened to these nontrial cases has been the great overlooked factor in our system. We are working on that factor now. We aim to increase the settlement ratio and, just as important, to provide earlier and cheaper ways of getting cases resolved.

We are using mediation by settlement judges and volunteer lawyers who serve without pay. We are making increased use of arbitration conducted outside the courthouse. We are monitoring cases from the beginning to make sure that the parties—while still having the right to a full trial if they want one—also have every chance to end the battle quickly and reasonably.

In this district a new committee has been appointed by the chief judge to improve our services in all these respects. The results will not be in the papers but they will be important.

Will the system of justice be saved? The question has to be asked as we face huge and unprecedented demands from the war on drugs, the ever-growing criminal calendar, and the burgeoning civil caseload.

Here are one man's gratuitous predictions for the balance of this century:

❑ The courts will be saved, largely through their own efforts.

❑ They will become much more innovative in offering alternative dispute resolution. People will come to court expecting not just the traditional battle, glorious though it is, but expecting and getting expert help in resolving their cases quickly by agreement.

❑ Plain English will take over as the language of the legal profession.

❑ The courts, and everybody else, will benefit from a growing recognition that crime must be reduced, not just by law enforcement but by eliminating its main and most obvious causes.

These are optimistic predictions, to be sure. But we have much reason for optimism, both in our people and in our institutions.

Every year, we federal judges see a new crop of young law graduates applying for clerkships in our chambers. They are superb. They are unmistakably smarter and wiser than we were at their age.

And every couple of months, as the naturalization judge, I get to swear in new citizens—sometimes, especially on the Fourth of July, as many as five hundred at a time. They come from all over the world—Poland, Ireland, Vietnam, the USSR, Egypt, Zambia, France, and scores of other countries. Their upturned faces are filled with cheer and confidence even as I read the baffling language of the oath:

> Do you hereby declare, on oath, that you absolutely and
> entirely renounce and abjure all allegiance and fidelity to any
> foreign prince, potentate, state, or sovereignty, of whom or
> which you have heretofore been a subject or citizen. . . .

To immigrants still working on English, that passage must be as mysterious as the Latin Mass. But, in talking to them afterward, it becomes clear that they know why they are here, and that this country's free legal institutions are among the main reasons.

Those of you who read the last Monday Club mailing may remember that the title of this paper was given as "Rumpole Was Right." You may wonder what the title has to do with what I have talked about. The title, of course, is not my fault. It is entirely the responsibility of Bob Heilman. Now that I think of it, he may have suggested: "Rumpole Was Wrong." However, I am very fond of Horace Rumpole, the crusty barrister who defends criminals at Old Bailey in John Mortimer's novels and television scripts. Rumpole usually is right, especially in the free use he makes of quotations from Shakespeare. I feel sure that he would agree with this critique of the law's delay and the insolence of office, and that he would now remind me: "Brevity is the soul of wit."

Thank you.

NOTES

1 The Monday Club is a group of well-known business and professional types that meets one Monday a month, generally at the Rainier Club in Seattle, to hear a speech or paper given by one of its number.

2 Robert B. Heilman (1907–2004) was chair of the University of Washington English Department from 1948 to 1971 and author of many significant works of literary scholarship. At the time of Heilman's death, Pat Soden, director of the University of Washington Press, which published several of Heilman's books, said, "Robert Heilman was one of the twentieth century's great literary voices and his scholarship will continue to inform future generations of students."

3 From 1974 to 1986, Donald S. Voorhees (1916–89) served as U. S. District Court judge for the Western District of Washington.

4 1 Corinthians 6:7.

5 Ambrose Bierce, *The Devil's Dictionary* (1911), p. 194.

6 Learned Hand, "The Deficiencies of Trials to Reach the Heart of the Matter" (1921) in *Lectures in Legal Topics* 3:89 (1926), p. 105.

7 Racketeer Influenced and Corrupt Organizations Act, Pub. Law 91–452 (codified at 18 U.S. C. §§ 1961–68).

Pro Bono's Triple Win

SPEECH PRESENTED FOR JUDGE DWYER

BY JOANNA DWYER

GOLDMARK AWARD LUNCHEON

LEGAL FOUNDATION OF WASHINGTON

February 21, 2002

I am Joanna Dwyer, Judge Dwyer's daughter. My father wanted very much to speak to you today, so he asked me to read these remarks as if he were delivering them himself. So, from this part on, the pronoun "I" will refer not to me but to my Dad.

I AM DEEPLY HONORED TO RECEIVE THIS AWARD. I know as well as anyone that others are much more deserving of it, but that will not deter me from accepting in the full spirit or from saying a few words to you about pro bono.

This award is especially gratifying because it bears the name of my late friend Chuck Goldmark, who stood for everything that is best in the legal profession. My wife and I and our children have had the good fortune to be close friends with three generations of Gold-marks—with John and Sally, who moved to this state from the East

Coast after World War II and took up a new life as ranchers; with their two sons, Chuck and Peter, and their wives; and with the new generation of Goldmarks, which we trust, will produce at least one lawyer to offset an unnecessarily high number of scientists.

The phrase "pro bono" endures as a rare survival of Latin in everyday legal talk. We don't hear much any more about *res ipsa loquitur* or *de minimis non curat lex*, but pro bono is here to stay as a shorthand way of referring to the providing of legal services without charge to those who cannot afford to pay for them. This activity of ours, it seems to me, is not a sideline, but is at the heart of our calling. It also represents a rare triple win—it benefits three distinct categories of people.

First, and most obviously, there is the client. Unequal access to justice remains a major problem in American life. About three-fourths of the legal needs of the poor go unmet because of the expense barrier, and our society as a whole has been unwilling to bridge the gap; the United States spends far less per capita on subsidized legal representation than the other Western industrial societies. Pro bono alone can't fill the entire need, but it can make a tremendous difference. The client, ordinarily, would go without legal help if it were not provided free of charge. Psychiatrists are fond of telling their patients that unless they pay the full freight they will not appreciate or value sufficiently the hours of consultation. I don't believe that has ever been a problem with free legal services. In my experience, the gratitude felt by those who receive pro bono legal help is almost boundless. Some of them even decide they want to go to law school, an impulse that should be carefully monitored.

Then there is the public. Let us remember that pro bono's full name is *pro bono publico*—for the good of the people. When the unrepresented gain legal assistance, it is not just they but all of us— all citizens and the entire legal system—who benefit. To the extent that access to justice is denied to any segment of society because of unequal wealth, we all suffer, because we know that life is only good in a society where justice is available to everyone, not just to a privileged few.

Finally, and most often overlooked, there are the lawyers themselves. Pro bono cases are fun—they often form the most interesting, exciting, and memorable parts of a legal career. Deborah Rhode, in her excellent recent book on the legal profession, writes, "The greatest source of discontent among today's lawyers is their perceived lack of contribution to social justice."[1] That feeling can easily be dispelled by pro bono.

I will mention as examples two Seattle lawyers who have brought honor to their profession, as well as happy memories to themselves, through their pro bono work:

Nancy Pacharzina I met quite recently when she worked as an extern in my chambers during her last year of law school. She graduated, passed the bar, served a clerkship in another district, and then joined a major law firm in Seattle. While there, she undertook a lawsuit on behalf of migratory farm workers. The goal was to require enforcement of the laws creating standards for the housing of these workers. Nancy put in something like 1,500 hours of work, and the suit succeeded. She is likely to have a long and successful career, but I doubt that she will ever have a more personally rewarding case than this one.

Matt Kenney I met many years ago, when he showed up as counsel for parties opposed to my clients in major commercial litigation. He still does that for a living—complex civil litigation—but he also devotes half of his working time to a legal aid clinic, where he gives advice and assistance to the poor. Matt is a pro bono hero because he gives his time and skill unselfishly to those who could never pay his bills at the usual rates.

These two lawyers have been exceptionally generous, but they also have been exceptionally rewarded. Similar rewards are open to every lawyer who is willing to donate time and work to those who need help most desperately.

Thank you.

NOTE

1 Deborah Rhode, *In the Interests of Justice: Reforming the Legal Profession* (New York: Oxford University Press, 2000).

Appendix

COMPILED BY MEADE EMORY

BOOKS BY WILLIAM L. DWYER

The Goldmark Case: An American Libel Trial. Seattle: University of Washington Press, 1984.[1]

In The Hands of the People: The Trial Jury's Origins, Triumphs, Troubles, and Future in American Democracy. New York: Thomas Dunne Books, St. Martin's Press, 2002.[2]

BAR ASSOCIATION REPORT BY WILLIAM DWYER, CHAIR

"Report of the Washington State Bar Association's Special Commission to Study and Report on the Antitrust Laws." Washington

State Bar Association, 1983. Introductory letter signed by Chair William L. Dwyer.

OTHER WRITINGS

"Protecting the Right of Trial by Jury; It Requires, and Is Worth, Vigilance," 25 *Trial* 77 (June 1989).

"How the American Legal System Can Be Saved from Itself." Speech by Dwyer to the City Club Forum in Seattle, Nov. 1, 1990. This is a thoughtful discourse on the state of the court system in this country. It can be obtained from the U.S. Courts Library at the United States Court House in Seattle.

"Introduction" to Emmett Watson's *Once Upon a Time in Seattle*. Seattle: Lesser Seattle Publishing, 1992.

"Proud to Be a Lawyer." Washington State Bar Association, website feature, May 31, 2004 (posthumous publication). *http://www.wsba .org/lawyers/links/proud/may31 04.htm*

HEARING TRANSCRIPTS

Committee for an Independent Post-Intelligencer. This organization was represented by William Dwyer during 1981–1983 in its capacity as Intervenor, urging denial of the application, in the Matter of the Application of the Seattle Times Company and the Hearst Corporation for Approval of a Joint Newspaper Operation Agreement.[3]

"Nomination of William L. Dwyer to be U. S. District Judge for the Western District of Washington," Confirmation Hearings on Federal Appointments, Committee on the Judiciary, United States Senate (Senate Hrg. 100–1009, Pt. 3). Hearing dates: Sept. 11, 1987, October 22,

1987. Contains much biographical material about Dwyer and expressions of support from many and varied quarters for his nomination.

"Hearings of the Commission on Structural Alternatives for the Federal Courts of Appeals," Seattle, May 27, 1998. This Commission was created by Congress to study the structure and alignment of the Federal appellate system with particular reference to the Ninth Circuit. In a hearing in Seattle presided over by Justice Byron White, Judge Dwyer (at p. 198) articulately states his conclusion that the Ninth Circuit functions well in its present size and format and that nothing is to be gained by "chopping up circuits."[4]

CONTINUING LEGAL EDUCATION MATERIALS

"Public Interest Law," sponsored by the Washington State Bar Association and the Seattle–King County Bar Association, 1973. Contains extensive materials on class actions by William L. Dwyer (with Richard C. Yarmuth).

"Antitrust Law," chaired by William L. Dwyer, sponsored by Washington State Bar Association, Section of Antitrust Law and Continuing Legal Education Committee, 1974. Materials contain Dwyer's "Introduction to the Antitrust Laws," followed by his foundational bibliography.

"William Dwyer's and Paul Luvera's Second Annual Northwest Trial Mastery Demonstration Program," June 16–21, 1997, University of Washington, Seattle

"Masters of the Criminal Practice," Murray Guterson, chair, with William Dwyer on the faculty. The materials contain Dwyer's "Cross-Examination Made Easy." Continuing Legal Education Committee of the Washington State Bar Association (1998).

"Charles Horowitz Lecture," November 10, 1988, presented by the Friends of the Washington Commission for the Humanities at the Museum of History and Industry, Seattle. Speaking on "justice" were William L. Dwyer, John Bridgman, and James M. Dolliver.

"Upholding the Promise—Profiles in Judicial Courage" (Alliance for Justice, 1996). Profiles four judges and the cases in which they made controversial decisions that adhered to judicial principles in the face of political pressure and extreme criticism from the public and the media. Judge William L. Dwyer is interviewed on the U.S. Forest Service's logging plans for spotted owl habitat.

Dedication of the William L. Dwyer Endowed Chair in Law at the University of Washington School of Law, and Installation of Professor Stewart M. Jay, June 28, 2001.

LEGAL PERIODICAL ARTICLES
ABOUT WILLIAM L. DWYER

"St. William the Just: A Sense of Place that Drives the Nemesis of the Logging Industry," 16 *The National Law Journal* 1 (June 20, 1994).

Letter to the Editor, by William Kirby, Olympia. *Washington State Bar News*, June 2002. Writer praises Judge Dwyer for "stoically staying at his post like a Roman," when he could have taken medical retirement because of Parkinson's disease. Noting his passing, the *Bar News* ran Judge Dwyer's picture on the cover of the March 2002 issue.[5]

Judge Barbara Jacobs Rothstein and Frederic C. Tausend, Esq., "Canary in the Coal Mine: The Importance of the Trial Jury," 26 *Seattle Uni-*

versity Law Review 395 (Winter 2003). Dedication of a Symposium Issue of the *Seattle University Law Review* to Judge Dwyer's vision of the jury as the guardian of our liberties.

Old Brompton Road v. Southern Comfort Foods, Inc.,
703 F. Supp. 879 (June 23, 1988)

In suit for copyright infringement, owners of songs under copyright entitled to damages for unauthorized performances of songs in a nightclub.

Pearl Jane Vanscoter et al. v. Otis R. Bowen, Secretary of U.S. Department of H.H.S., 706 F. Supp. 1432 (July 14, 1988)

Action brought by parents of minor children claiming there were deficiencies in federal regulations governing treatment of "pass-through payments" (amounts received by the state's Office of Support Enforcement [OSE] from absent parents). Court held regulations violate Social Security Act with plaintiffs being entitled to receive up to $50 of each support payment whether or not *actually* collected by the OSE in the month in which it is due.

Harold D. Whitehead et al. v. Thomas Turnage, Administrator of the Veterans Administration, 701 F. Supp. 795 (July 21, 1988)

Class of past, present, and future mortgagers under a Veterans Administration loan program sought retroactive application of a case (*U.S. v. Vallejo,* 660 F. Supp. 536 [W.D. Wash, 1967]) holding that the Administration could not collect a deficiency judgment pursuant to nonjudicial foreclosure. Court held that the case would be retroactively applied but relief would be limited by the federal statute of limitations for bringing claims against the United States.

Joan Brown v. Jack Kemp, Secretary of Department of Housing & Urban Development et al., 714 F. Supp. 445 (May 12, 1989)

Plaintiff, a business woman, after falling behind in a FHA loan, brought action against HUD to compel it to refinance her loan under a Department program. The court disagreed with the Department's conclusion that plaintiff's default was not caused by circumstances beyond her control and its conclusion that there was not a reasonable prospect that she would be able to resume and complete payments as required. Finding that neither conclusion was supported by the record or HUD's own regulations, the court held that the Department's rejection of mortgagor's application was arbitrary and capricious.

Coral Construction Company v. King County, 729 F. Supp. 734 (December 4, 1989)

Construction company brought action against county challenging its set-aside program for minority and women-owned business enterprises (MWBE). On cross motions for summary judgment, the court held that the program did not violate the equal protection clause.

Gregory H. Bowers v. James Jura, Administrator of the U.S. Department of Energy, Bonneville Power Administration, 749 F. Supp. 1049 (June 8, 1990)

In a suit by a professional engineer seeking review of decision by Bonneville Power Administration (BPA) to proceed with high voltage electric transmission project to increase capability of transferring power between Pacific Northwest and California, court held that the Court of Appeals had original jurisdiction to consider lawsuit challenging final action of BPA.

Valerie Cunningham et al. v. Municipality of Metropolitan Seattle (METRO) et al., 751 F. Supp. 885 (September 6, 1990)

Voters living in parts of King County that were allegedly underrepresented on the governing council of METRO brought action challenging the method by which the council was selected. The court determined that METRO had governmental powers and that the majority of its members were elected, thus making the "one person, one vote" principle applicable (which principle holds that no person's vote may be reduced in value compared to the votes of others because of where they happen to live) and, further, that the current method of electing the council violated that principle.

Ralph A. Erickson et al. v. United States, 780 F. Supp. 733 (September 13, 1990)

Taxpayers brought a suit challenging IRS tax liens under which their personal and real property was seized and sold. The defendant's motion to dismiss the case noted that the Anti-Injunction Act barred any action seeking to enjoin the IRS from enforcing a lien or sale. A statute (28 U.S.C. § 2410) pursuant to which the United States could be joined in a quiet title action affecting property upon which the U.S. "claimed a lien" would not, the court held, serve as a basis for jurisdiction since the property was sold more than two years ago.

Valerie Cunningham v. Municipality of Metropolitan Seattle (METRO) et al., 751 F. Supp. 899 (November 28, 1990)

Following the decision in Cunningham v. METRO, above, the court held that state and local officials would be given until the end of the

1992 legislative session (some 16 months) to devise a constitutionally acceptable method.

Kwan Fai Mak v. James Blodgett, 754 F. Supp. 1490 (Jan 8, 1990)

After defendant's conviction and sentence to death for participating in the murders of thirteen people were affirmed by Washington Supreme Court, he sought habeas corpus. The court held that
petitioner's conviction on all counts of aggravated first-degree murder was constitutionally valid. Petition for writ of habeas corpus was
denied insofar as it sought a new trial as to guilt or innocence. Since,
however, petitioner's counsel failed to present available mitigating
evidence at his sentencing hearing, petitioner was deprived of his
6th Amendment right to effective assistance of counsel. Petition
therefore granted as to sentence of death, which sentence was
vacated.

Seattle Audubon Society et al. v. John L. Evans et al.,
771 F. Supp. 1081 (May 23, 1991)

The court had previously entered (on March 7, 1991) an order on
summary judgment declaring unlawful a proposal by the Forest Service to permit logging northern spotted owl habitat areas located in
Washington, Oregon, and Northern California as not in compliance
with the National Forest Management Act (NFMA). Plaintiffs
moved for a permanent injunction prohibiting the sale of logging
rights in additional spotted owl habitat areas until the Forest Service complies with the NFMA by adopting standards and guidelines
to assure that a viable population of the species is maintained in the
forests. Permanent injunction granted and Forest Service enjoined
to proceed diligently in compliance with the NFMA and to submit
to the court (and to have in effect by March 5, 1992) revised stan-

dards and guidelines to insure the northern spotted owl's viability, together with an environmental impact statement (EIS) as required by the NFMA.[6]

Seattle Audubon Society et al. v. James R. Moseley et al.,
798 F. Supp. 1473 (May 28, 1992)

Pursuant to the order in *Evans* (above), the Forest Service prepared and issued a new EIS. The Department of Agriculture (Moseley) adopted the Forest Service's preferred alternative from the EIS. Here plaintiff challenges the legality of the EIS, alleging it fails to assess the environmental consequences to the northern spotted owl of continued logging of its habitat and does not assure the viability of the owl and other old growth dependent species, all in violation of the NFMA. The court held that the Forest Service had not complied with the National Environmental Policy Act (NEPA), in that it lacked reasoned discussion of major scientific objectives and that it must take further action under the statute.

Seattle Audubon Society, et al. v. James R. Moseley et al.,
798 F. Supp. 1484 (July 2, 1992)

Further proceedings in the challenge to the legality of the final EIS issued by the Forest Service in response to *Evans* (above). Court held that the Forest Service could not adopt a management plan for owls that it knew or believed would result in extirpation of other vertebrate species, and, therefore, injunctive relief was warranted, including a requirement that Forest Service prepare a new or supplemental EIS in compliance with NEPA. Court also held that Forest Service could not auction or award any additional timber sales that would log suitable habitat for owl until revised standards and guidelines were adopted and in effect.

Seattle Audubon Society et al. v. James R. Moseley et al.,
798 F. Supp. 1494 (July 21, 1992)

Forest Service and Washington Contract Loggers Association (defendant-intervenor) moved for stay of injunction pending appeal. Held: stay of pending appeal was not justified for portion of injunction prohibiting Forest Service from auctioning or awarding additional timber sales in owl's habitat; stay pending appeal was not warranted for portion of injunction directing Forest Service to prepare new or supplemental EIS. A period of eight months, in addition to the five months required for statutory comment, publication, and waiting periods, was reasonable for Forest Service to complete process for issuance of new statement.

Jerry Edmon Fordyce v. City of Seattle, 840 F. Supp. 784
(July 29, 1993)

An action was brought against city and eight of its police officers by plaintiff who was arrested while videotaping public demonstration. On motions for summary judgment, court held (i) police officers were entitled to qualified immunity based on reasonable belief that it was lawful to arrest plaintiff for having recorded private conversations in violation of a Washington statute; (ii) city entitled to dismissal of § 1983 claims (liability for deprivation of civil rights, etc.) absent evidence that a failure to train police officers occurred or that policy of city itself caused deprivation of constitutional rights; and (iii) judgment rendered that statute in question (RCW 9.73.030) does not prohibit recording of conversation held in public street, within earshot of passersby, by means of readily apparent recording device. Following appeal to the Ninth Circuit, on remand from that court, see 907 F. Supp. 1446 (Dec. 5, 1995).

Susan Thorsted et al. v. Christine O. Gregoire et al.,
841 F. Supp. 1068 (February 10, 1994)

State law approved by voters through initiative in 1992 by means of Initiative 573 prevented incumbents who had served for a specified number of years from winning reelection to the U.S. Senate or House of Representatives. Voters and a congressional representative (Rep. Thomas Foley) sought declaratory judgment enjoining Secretary of State and Attorney General from enforcing provisions of resulting state law. Held: Voters' freedom to choose federal legislators must not be abridged by laws that make qualified people ineligible to serve. In adopting a short but comprehensive list of qualifications for Congress—age, citizenship, and residency—the Framers protected the indisputable right of the people to return whom they thought proper. The law violates the qualification clauses of the Constitution by imposing a new qualification, i.e., nonincumbency beyond a specified period. While applicable law permits a prevailing party ordinarily to recover attorney's fees, such is not the case when "special circumstances" would make such an award unjust. Among others, such special circumstances include the fact that the legislation prompting the suit was adopted by the voters not by state officials.

Seattle Audubon Society et al. v. James Lyons et al.,
871 F. Supp. 1286 (August 5, 1994)

In consolidated cases concerning environmental groups' challenge to federal management of land containing spotted owl habitat, Secretaries of Agriculture and Interior, Forest Service, Bureau of Land Management and related officials sought leave to assert cross-claims against Northwest Forest Research Council (NFRC). Held: (i) federal defendants had standing to assert declaratory judgment cross-claims against NFRC; (ii) federal defendants would be granted leave to plead cross-claims against NFRC; and (iii) motion for joinder of NFRC's co-plaintiffs in separate case as additional parties is denied and such co-plaintiffs are given leave to intervene.

In Re Immunex Securities Litigation, 864 F. Supp. 142
(August 29, 1994)

Counsel for plaintiffs and class members sought attorney fees in securities class action. Court held that contingent fee should be based on net, not gross, recovery after costs are deducted. Awarding 30 percent of net recovery was reasonable when checked against lodestar amount with multiplier for risk. The lodestar amount would be the fee for work done if charged at current hourly rates. A percentage fee produced by multiplying the lodestar amount by 1.6 for risk was determined to be reasonable.

United States v. Duane B. McCaslin, 863 F. Supp. 1299
(September 2, 1994)

After defendant's property was forfeited based on its use to facilitate drug offenses, defendant was convicted and sentenced for the offenses underlying the forfeiture. Raising the issue of double jeopardy, defendant moved to vacate conviction and sentence. Multiple punishments are permissible if imposed in the same proceeding, barred if imposed in a separate proceeding. Civil forfeiture of property used to facilitate a drug offense is "punishment." Forfeiture and criminal sanctions arose out of separate proceedings. Defendant unconstitutionally subjected to a second punishment for same offense in separate proceeding when convicted and sentenced, thus requiring vacation of criminal conviction and sentence.

Seattle Audubon Society et al. v. James Lyons et al.,
871 F. Supp. 1291 (December 21, 1994)

In consolidated cases, environmental groups and timber industry association challenged legality of forest management plan adopted by U.S.
Secretaries of Agriculture and Interior. Plaintiffs and federal defendants filed cross-motions for summary judgment against each other.
Court found that the federal defendants had acted within the lawful
scope of their discretion in adopting the 1994 forest plan. Plaintiffs'
motion for summary judgment denied and federal defendants' cross-
motions for summary judgment granted.

Mark A. Philips v. William Perry et al., 883 F. Supp. 539
(March 17, 1995)

Navy service member brought action seeking injunction to prevent
his discharge from service. Parties filed cross-motions for summary
judgment. Service member may not be discharged solely because of
homosexual status but may be because of homosexual acts. Navy's
regulation in that regard is constitutional but that does not mean it
is wise (e.g., often results in the loss of individuals who serve with
great honor and distinction). Defendant's motion for summary judgment is granted.

Sprint Spectrum, L.P., v. City of Medina, 924 F. Supp. 1036
(May 3, 1996)

Wireless communications service provider brought action against city,
challenging city resolution establishing six-month moratorium on
issuance of new special use permits for wireless communication facilities and seeking injunction and damages. Held: (i) moratorium did
not have a prohibiting effect but was, rather, a short-term suspen-

sion of permit issuing while city gathered information and processed application (Tel. Comm. Act of 1996 does not intend to force local government procedures into rigid timetables when circumstances call for study); (ii) OBRA of 1992, providing that no local government shall have authority to regulate entry of mobile service, was not violated since city did not regulate entry.

Covington Greens Associates II et al. v. Covington Water District et al., 931 F. Supp. 738 (June 26, 1996)

Real estate developers brought action in state court against water district and board members, alleging they were unlawfully denied water meters and connections. Defendants removed action to federal court. Held: District's challenged actions were legislative in nature (i.e., general enactments directed to overall problem of water shortage, which actions were performed in the normal manner prescribed by law). Actions in response to water shortage were lawful under test guarding against arbitrary and capricious government action.

Idaho Sportsmen's Coalition et al. v. Carol Browner et al., 951 F. Supp. 962 (September 26, 1996)

Citizen's suit brought under the Clean Water Act (CWA) to compel EPA to perform duties required by CWA toward ridding Idaho's water bodies of pollution. EPA moved to dismiss and plaintiffs moved for order establishing total maximum daily load (TMDL) schedule. (TMDLs are the greatest amount of pollution the water body can receive daily without violating state's water quality standards.) Idaho's proposed schedule for TMDL development violated CWA in its extreme slowness. (The CWA requires the identification of waters which are water quality limited, followed by a priority ranking of those waters requiring the strongest TMDL limits.) Rather than identify a specific schedule, court held that the appropriate remedy is to remand to EPA for exercise of its discretion to revise and reissue proper schedule.

Idaho Conservation League v. Carol Browner, 968 F. Supp. 546
(February 20, 1997)

Environmental groups filed citizen suit under the Clean Water Act (CWA) against the EPA for relief from the EPA's alleged violation of the CWA for failure to approve or disapprove state's water quality standards (WQS) or upon disapproval for failing to promulgate substitute standards. On motions for summary judgment court held: (i) CWA imposed mandatory duty on EPA to prepare and publish proposed regulations to meet CWA standards for WQS and that failure to do so could be challenged in a citizen suit; (ii) a delay of seven months established that EPA as a matter of law failed to perform its mandatory duty under the CWA; and (iii) the EPA's failure to carry out its duties under the EPA was arbitrary, capricious, and not in accordance with law, and thus in violation of the Administrative Procedure Act (APA).

John Doe v. Christine O. Gregoire, 960 F. Supp. 1478
(March 21, 1997)

Convicted sex offender brought § 1983 suit seeking injunction prohibiting enforcement of Washington's Community Protection Act of 1990. Held: (i) the ex post facto clause prohibited enforcement of the public notification provisions of the Act as such provisions were punitive and not merely regulatory (thereby prohibiting enforcement against a sex offender convicted of crimes predating enactment of the Act); (ii) provisions of the Act requiring registration of convicted sex offenders and notification of law enforcement agencies were regulatory and not punitive, thus the ex post facto clause did not preclude application to offenses committed prior to enactment of Act.

GTE Northwest, Inc., v. Sharon L. Nelson et al., 969 F. Supp. 654
(March 31, 1997)

Incumbent telephone local exchange carrier (LEC) brought action against carrier seeking to enter market, challenging arbitrator's order which had been incorporated into interconnection agreement submitted for approval to the Washington Utilities and Transportation Commission (WUTC). Action brought under Telecommunications Act of 1996 which sets forth detailed requirements for the development of an interconnection agreement between an incumbent and a provider seeking to enter the market. Considering the Act in its entirety, it is clear, the court held, that Congress intended to defer court review until an agreement has become final. Since it has not, the motion to dismiss was granted.

Daniel Hagy v. United States et al., 976 F. Supp. 1373
(May 6, 1997)

Alleging wrongful death of his wife resulting from a human growth hormone treatment she received as a child under a program funded by federal grants, plaintiff sued under the Federal Tort Claims Act (FTCA). Hormones were received by decedent under a program under which the NIH awarded Johns Hopkins University grants that provided funding for the National Hormone and Pituitary Program (NHPP). Defendant moved to dismiss for lack of jurisdiction under the FTCA. Court held that defendant was protected from liability under two exceptions to FTCA applicability. The "independent contractor" exception applied since the contaminated hormones came from such a contractor, not the government. Simply because the NIH had the ability to compel contractor's compliance does not change the contractor's personnel into federal employees. Under the "discretionary function" exception the United States is not liable for claims based on the exercise (or failure to exercise) or performance of a discretionary function. There was no directive requiring warning with respect to the hormones, thus any decision not to warn was discretionary.

Reginald L. Kees et al. v. Arthur Wallenstein et al.,
973 F. Supp. 1191 (May 14, 1997)

Former county correctional officers brought action against county and county officials alleging § 1983, Americans with Disabilities Act (ADA), Washington Law against Discrimination (WLAD), and intentional and negligent infliction of emotional distress claims under Washington law. Each had suffered an injury or other medical problem that prevented them from having direct contacts with inmates, causing them to be assigned to light duty, control room, etc. After attempts were made to find them other positions, they were terminated. In ruling on motions for summary judgment, the court noted that for ADA relief plaintiffs must show they are disabled within the ADA and that they are qualified to perform job functions. Since the ability to handle the inmates under various circumstances is an essential function of the position, inability of the plaintiffs to have direct contact with the inmates because of their disability results in their being "not qualified" within the ADA or WLAD. Further, officials were entitled to qualified immunity from former correctional officer's § 1983 claims.

US West Communications, Inc., v. TCG Seattle et al.,
971 F. Supp. 1365 (July 24, 1997)

Plaintiff incumbent local exchange carrier (LEC) sought review of determinations made by Washington Utilities and Transportation Commission (WUTC) in approving interconnection agreement between carriers under Telecommunications Act of 1996. WUTC commissioners moved to dismiss. Court held that United States was entitled to intervene as a matter of right to defend constitutionality of grant of authority by Telecommunications Act to review by state commission. FCC has no statutory entitlement to intervention; in defending constitutionality of the Act, it would be adequately represented. By participating in interconnection agreement process the state of Washington waived its immunity from federal judicial review of its actions.

Francisco Pastor-Camarena v. Richard Smith et al.,
977 F. Supp. 1415 (July 24, 1997)

Illegal alien who was in custody of INS filed petition for writ of habeas corpus, seeking order releasing him from custody pending deportation proceedings against him. The court held that the alien was not required to exhaust his administrative remedies if to do so would be futile; the BIA had recently interpreted the statutory provision in question in an *en banc* proceeding (therefore there was no reason to believe the result would be different if petitioner first presented his challenge to the BIA). The court held that the alien was eligible for release on bond despite his prior incarceration.

Patrick Getty et al. v. Philip Steven Harmon et al.,
53 F. Supp. 2nd 1053 (April 1, 1999)

In a securities fraud action brought under § 10(b) and Rule 10b-5 of Securities Exchange Act of 1934, defendants moved for summary judgment on grounds that the claims were time barred. Under § 10(b) a complaint must be filed within one year after the discovery of facts constituting the violation (and within three years after such violation, the statute of repose). The period is triggered when a plaintiff is on inquiry notice of facts constituting a violation (i.e., facts that would lead a reasonable person to investigate and acquire actual knowledge of the defendant's misrepresentations). Since there was no uncontroverted evidence that plaintiff discovered, or should have discovered, no fraudulent acts on the part of the defendant, there are issues of fact as to when complainants were on inquiry notice, thereby requiring denial of defendant's motion for summary judgment. With respect to the three-year statute of repose, since buyers had the option of rejecting renewal, each renewal of securities started the running of new statute of repose.

Khamsaene Sivongxay v. Janet Reno, 56 F.Supp. 2nd 1085 (July 9, 1999)

Alien filed petition for habeas corpus challenging his continued detention pending deportation. Held: (i) since the postdeportation detention scheme of Illegal Immigration Reform & Immigrant Responsibility Act (IIRIRA) does not apply retroactively, alien could not be held for more than the allowable pre-IIRIRA six-month period, and (ii) continued detention of alien pending deportation to the country that refused him admittance violated his substantive due process rights since it was unlikely that he would be deported in the near future. Petition granted.

Northwest Laborers–Employers Health and Safety Trust Fund v. Philip Morris Incorporated, 58 F. Supp. 2nd 1211 (July 22, 1999)

Plaintiffs are collectively-bargained-for health and welfare trusts. Plaintiffs alleged conspiracy by defendants to deceive and defraud the health care providers by misrepresenting the addictiveness of tobacco, etc. On defendants' motion for summary judgment, held: (i) the injuries suffered by health and welfare plans were too remote from companies' misconduct in marketing sales of tobacco to require damages under Washington Consumer Protection Act (the individual smokers were more direct victims of the alleged wrongdoing); (ii) under Washington law, companies did not interfere with contractual relations absent evidence that the companies knew of the funds or their contractual relations with their beneficiaries. Motion granted.

Oregon Natural Resources Council Action et al. v. U.S. Forest Service and Bureau of Land Management et al., 59 F. Supp. 2nd 1085 (August 2, 1999)

Environmental groups challenged timber sales by the U.S. Forest Service. Held: (i) defendant's exemption of several timber sales from forest management plan requirement that wildlife surveys be conducted for activities implemented after certain date was contrary to plain language of record of decision under which plan was issued, (ii) while a supplemental environmental impact statement (SEIS) is required if the agency makes substantial changes in the proposed plan that are relevant to environmental concerns, the Forest Service's failure to conduct a SEIS prior to approving timber sales was not arbitrary and capricious absent showing that new information could not be addressed under existing forest management plan.

Ramiro Prado Hernandez v. Janet Reno et al., 86 F. Supp. 2nd 1037 (August 3, 1999)

Alien petitioned for writ of habeas corpus contending that it was unlawful for the INS to reinstate his prior order of deportation without a hearing and without first acting on his application for adjustment of status. Held: the alien who reentered the country illegally after prior order of deportation was not prohibited from seeking adjustment to lawful permanent status (in this case because of marriage to a U.S. citizen) by virtue of section of Immigration Nationality Act providing that prior order of removal is reinstated and not subject to being reopened or reviewed when alien has reentered the U.S. after having been removed. The request for adjudication of his status did not constitute a challenge to the prior order of deportation. Petition granted.

Richard Turay v. Mark Seling, PhD, et al., 108 F. Supp. 2nd 1148
(May 5, 2000)

Sexually violent predators, civilly committed by state, challenged conditions of confinement as violating due process. Consolidated cases involved conditions of confinement at the Special Commitment Center at McNeil Island, Washington. Held: Although state had made progress, it continued to make constitutionally inadequate mental health treatment available, which treatment did not provide those committed a realistic opportunity for improvement. Court retained jurisdiction to monitor progress.

SELECTED NEWSPAPER ARTICLES
ABOUT JUDGE DWYER

"The Law and Mr. Dwyer: U.S. Judgeship Candidate's Modesty Belies High Praise from Colleagues," Carol Ostrom, *The Seattle Times*, March 14, 1986, p. E1

"Dwyer: He's Bright, Honest and Not Yet a Judge," Emmett Watson, *The Seattle Times*, June 21, 1987, p. D1

"Dwyer Wrapped in Praise as He Dons a Federal Robe," Peyton Whitely, *The Seattle Times*, December 2, 1987, p. H1

"Judge Blocks Tree Harvest in 374,000 Acres: Blame Log Exports, Not the Spotted Owl Says Dwyer," David Schaefer & Bill Dietrich, *The Seattle Times*, March 16, 1989, p. C11

"Both Sides Say Owl-Habitat Case Is Critical," Bill Dietrich, *The Seattle Times*, May 5, 1991, p. B1

"William Dwyer: A Federal Judge Who Relishes the Tough

Cases," Steve Miletich, *Seattle Post-Intelligencer*, April 17, 1992, p. A1

"Fleshed-Out Timber Plan Up to Judge: Dwyer Must Decide If It Meets Environmental Law," Eric Pryne, *The Seattle Times*, July 17, 1993, p. A1

"From Trees to Term Limits, Dwyer Having Major Impact," Eric Pryne, *The Seattle Times*, April 12, 1994, p. A1

"District Judge William Dwyer: The Last Pages of a Controversial Career," Barbara Serrano, *The Seattle Times*, January 10, 1999, p. A1

"Judge Believes That 12 Heads Better Than One," Joel Connelly, *Seattle Post-Intelligencer*, December 24, 2001, p. A2

"Dwyer Not Afraid to Make Hard Decisions," Sarah Duran, *Tacoma News Tribune*, February 11, 2002, p A1

"Judge William Dwyer Dies: Legal Career Encompassed Spotted Owls, Baseball," Steve Miletich, *The Seattle Times*, February 13, 2002, p. A1

NOTES

1 Selected book reviews of *The Goldmark Case* are: Robert W. Critchlow, 21 *Gonzaga Law Review* 859 (Oct. 1986); John N. Rupp, 9 *University of Puget Sound Law Review* 585 (Spring, 1986); Carol T. Rieger, 3 *Constitutional Commentary* 266 (Winter, 1986); Maurice A. Frank, 130 *Chicago Daily Law Bulletin* 2 (Dec. 20, 1984); Douglas S. Lavine, 70 *ABA Journal* 100 (Nov. 1984).

A complete bound record of newspaper clippings relating to the Goldmark libel trial (from the *Wenatchee Daily World, Seattle Daily Times,* and *Seattle Post-Intelligencer*) is located at the U.W. Law Library, Special Collections. Also, the complete trial transcript of Goldmark vs. Canwell, et al., acc.1421–001, is available at the University of Washington Library, Special Collections.

2 Selected book reviews of *In the Hands of the People* are: Steve Weinberg, 25 *Legal Times* 25 (Jan. 28, 2002); Philip A. Talmadge, 25 *Seattle University Law Review* 541 (Winter, 2002); Jeffrey White, 38 *Trial* 76 (Feb. 2002); Steve Weinberg, 168 *New Jersey Law Journal* (May 20, 2002); Martin K. Schmidt, 75 *Wisconsin Lawyer* 30 (November, 2002); Jason Mazzone, 87 *Judicature* 40 (July-August, 2003).

3 The entire record of this proceeding, catalogued under "Committee for an Independent Post-Intelligencer" (acc. 3674) is located at the University of Washington Library, Special Collections. It consists of seven boxes: Box 1, Historical; Boxes 1–3, Hearing transcript before Admin. Law Judge; Box 4, Pleadings before Admin. Law Judge, post-hearing recommendation and conclusions; Box 5, Opinion and order of U.S. Attorney General; Box 6, Pleadings in U.S. District Court; Box 7, Pleadings in U.S. Court of Appeals and U.S. Supreme Court.

4 Hearing available on-line: http://www.library.unt.edu/gpo/csafca/hearings/seatrans.pdf

5 The WSBA News observed that he was "noted for decisions grounded in the most sophisticated social and biological science" and that his "life was a bridge between the nineteenth and twenty-first centuries."

6 Judge Dwyer's decisions in the spotted owl cases, of which this case is an example, prompted a good deal of controversy. See, e.g., from this listing, "St. William the Just: A Sense of Place that Drives the Nemesis of the Logging Industry" and "Upholding the Promise: Profiles in Judicial Courage," a video interview with Judge Dwyer on the Forest Service's logging plans for spotted owl habitat areas.

The logging community was so vocal on this issue that it attempted to have an impact on Judge Dwyer's handling of the cases (the opinions in several of these spotted owl cases were not, like most of those listed above, reported in the Federal Supplement). In 1989, in order to provide a short-term supply of timber for mills in Washington and Oregon, U.S. Senators

Hatfield and Adams proposed a rider to the fiscal year 1990 Interior Department Appropriations that set one-year overall target levels in the forest stands for the northern spotted owl; compliance with the rider's provisions would satisfy all relevant environmental statutes. The rider mentioned pending U.S. District Court cases, including those pending with Judge Dwyer. After this provision was enacted (Pub. Law 101–21, §318), its constitutionality was challenged on the ground that, in violation of separation of powers principles, it attempted to direct a particular judicial result. In *Robertson, Chief of U.S. Forest Service, et al. v. Seattle Audubon Society et al.*, 503 U.S. 429 (1992), the Supreme Court upheld the rider, finding that the legislation changed existing law rather than results under preexisting law.

A similar effort was made in 1995 by attaching a rider to an emergency appropriation for that year, again aimed at decisions Judge Dwyer had made or might make. The Emergency Salvage Timber Sale Program (ESTSP) directed the Forest Service to initiate salvage timber sales in named national forests in Washington and Oregon. Like the earlier rider, it overrode all preexisting environmental laws by providing that compliance with the rider's provisions was deemed sufficient to comply with all environmental statutes. However, it went beyond the earlier rider by providing approval of all sales "notwithstanding" any judicial decision, restraining order, or injunction issued prior to the legislation's enactment (Pub. Law 104–19, §2000[b][1]). Although not specifically attacked in the courts, the 1995 rider has been criticized by scholars as further upsetting the separation of powers by directing "specific results by reference to past actions taken by executive agencies, without changing the underlying laws." See Zellmer, "Sacrificing Legislative Integrity at the Altar of Appropriation Riders: A Constitutional Crisis," 21 *Harvard Environmental Law Rev.* 457, 525 (1997).

Acknowledgments

WHEN IT WAS LEARNED THAT JUDGE WILLIAM Dwyer had decided not to leave his papers in the public domain, the gloom accompanying his death was made even darker. Dwyer's reputation as a writer of remarkable prose was such that a literary legacy might, in some small way, have brightened a world without his presence. The darkness was pierced by a shaft of light when Judge Dwyer's widow, Vasiliki Dwyer, came forth with a manuscript of speeches given by Bill during his life, which Bill himself had assembled and hoped one day would be read and enjoyed by his grandchildren. While this small collection of vintage Dwyer may be less than we might have wanted to preserve from his pen, it will, to a great extent, serve as a reminder of who Bill Dwyer was, how appealingly thoughtful he was, and how eloquent and memorable his words were.

Once the existence of the Dwyer manuscript became known, I

focused on ensuring its wide dissemination. With an expression of interest in the project from the University of Washington Press, I sought to rally support from the University of Washington School of Law. Its dean, Joe Knight, initially endorsed the project. This was followed by financial assistance from the Law School's Graduate Program in Taxation. Professor Sam Donaldson, my successor as director, can be profoundly thanked for that assistance.

My affection for Bill and for his literary gifts prompted me to get behind preparing the manuscript for publication. Since an early decision was made to publish Bill's speeches exactly as he had left them, there wasn't much to "edit." There was, nevertheless, the task of enlisting an introduction and preparing whatever explanatory material the book was to contain. The speeches—only one of which preceded his nomination to the federal judicial bench—are devoid of legalese in need of clarification, but they do contain references to people and events that require some identification if the reader is to gain the full flavor of what Bill Dwyer said. Some of that desired context could be achieved through the use of endnote annotation, and in this task—as well as many, many others in connection with this book—I received unstinting and expert assistance from the U.W. Law Library's Reference Office, especially from the Assistant Librarian for Reference Services, Mary Whisner, under whose direction the research was done.

One of the very pleasing aspects of this collection is that these speeches were personally chosen by Judge Dwyer. During his life, especially after he went on the bench, there were few speakers in this area in greater demand than Bill Dwyer. Certainly Bill made some speeches he chose not to include, but those chosen are spread well across his period on the federal bench and were presented to a variety of audiences. My research turned up only two additional speeches that could well have been included. On November 1, 1990, Bill gave a speech before the City Club Forum in Seattle entitled "How the American Legal System Can Be Saved from Itself." Those interested in his view in 1990, three years after he went on the bench, of the state of the court system in this country and how it might better meet the demand for its services can read this valuable document in the U.S. Courts Library in the federal courthouse in Seattle. Also worthy of note is Judge Dwyer's "Eulogy for Donald S. Voorhees," given on July 18, 1989. The personal tone Judge Dwyer used on this occasion becomes readily understandable when it is known that he assumed Judge Voorhees's seat on the bench for the Western District of Washington when he was sworn in on December 1, 1987. That talk is also available in Seattle's U.S. Courts Library.

Most people who are familiar with Judge Dwyer's record know that he wrote two books during his career (*The Goldmark Case* and *In the Hands of the People*), both very well received and together constituting a significant literary legacy. These books could simply be listed in a bibliography, but readers of this volume are likely to want to know more about the author of the speeches. While it is clear that *Ipse Dixit* is not a biography, it appeared that a biographical aspect could be added by means of a detailed listing of books, articles, videos, continuing legal education materials, published judicial opinions, etc., written by and about Bill Dwyer. I was gratified to see several resources at the University of Washington Law Library that speak loudly of Dwyer's skill as a lawyer before he assumed the bench, specifically the full transcript of the Goldmark trial and the complete record of Dwyer's valiant representation of the "Committee for an Independent Post-Intelligencer," aimed at blocking, in the early 1980s, the Seattle newspaper Joint Operating Agreement.

There are several *individuals* whose devoted attention to this worthwhile project merit undying gratitude. Stimson Bullitt, a close friend of Judge Dwyer (note Dwyer's speech on the occasion of Bullitt's receipt of the Seattle-King County First Citizen Award), when asked to prepare an Introduction to this volume, did so with alacrity and eloquence. Vasiliki Dwyer submitted the collection of speeches for publication and was generous with her help on personal and editorial questions as the manuscript was being prepared. Certainly no one was in a better position to know how Bill Dwyer would have wanted his speeches preserved. Ron Hjorth, the dean emeritus of the School of Law, valued his friendship with Judge Dwyer and was very appreciative of all that Bill did for the School of Law, a circumstance that made Dean Hjorth a valuable mentor during work on the book. Special thanks to Marilyn Trueblood, managing editor at the University of Washington Press, and to Pat Soden, the Press's director, who comprehended from the beginning the merit and importance of the collected speeches of Bill Dwyer and whose regular encouragement of the project never faltered.

Meade Emory